German (17th-century).

ARMS AND ARMOR

A PICTORIAL ARCHIVE FROM NINETEENTH-CENTURY SOURCES

SELECTED AND ARRANGED BY

Carol Belanger Grafton

DOVER PUBLICATIONS, INC.

NEW YORK

Copyright

Copyright © 1995 by Dover Publications, Inc.
All rights reserved under Pan American and International Copyright Conventions.

Published in Canada by General Publishing Company, Ltd., 30 Lesmill Road, Don Mills, Toronto, Ontario.
Published in the United Kingdom by Constable and Company, Ltd., 3 The Lanchesters, 162–164 Fulham Palace Road, London W6 9ER.

Bibliographical Note

Arms and Armor: A Pictorial Archive from Nineteenth-Century Sources is a new work, first published by Dover Publications, Inc., in 1995.

DOVER *Pictorial Archive* SERIES

Library of Congress Cataloging-in-Publication Data

Arms and armor : a pictorial archive from nineteenth-century sources / selected and arranged by Carol Belanger Grafton.
    p.   cm. — (Dover pictorial archive series)
  ISBN 0-486-28561-8 (pbk.)
  1. Armor—History—Pictorial works. 2. Weapons—History—Pictorial works. I. Grafton, Carol Belanger. II. Series.
U800.A76 1995
623.4′41—dc20
                                                  95–16757
                                                     CIP

Manufactured in the United States of America
Dover Publications, Inc., 31 East 2nd Street, Mineola, N.Y. 11501

PUBLISHER'S NOTE

For better or worse, warfare is one of mankind's defining tendencies. Coercion by organized violence has played a crucial role in human life since prehistory, and the need for battlefield advantages has provided a continual impetus to the development of science and technology.

This book contains over 700 illustrations covering the history of weapons and armor in primarily the preindustrial West from ancient times until the eighteenth century, with a particular emphasis on European cultures of the Medieval and Renaissance periods. The contents are arranged chronologically, and each plate has a caption identifying nationality and date of origin, where known. Four plates of nonspecific decorative illustrations incorporating motifs from the periods covered are included at the end of the book.

Greek, Roman and Egyptian. 1

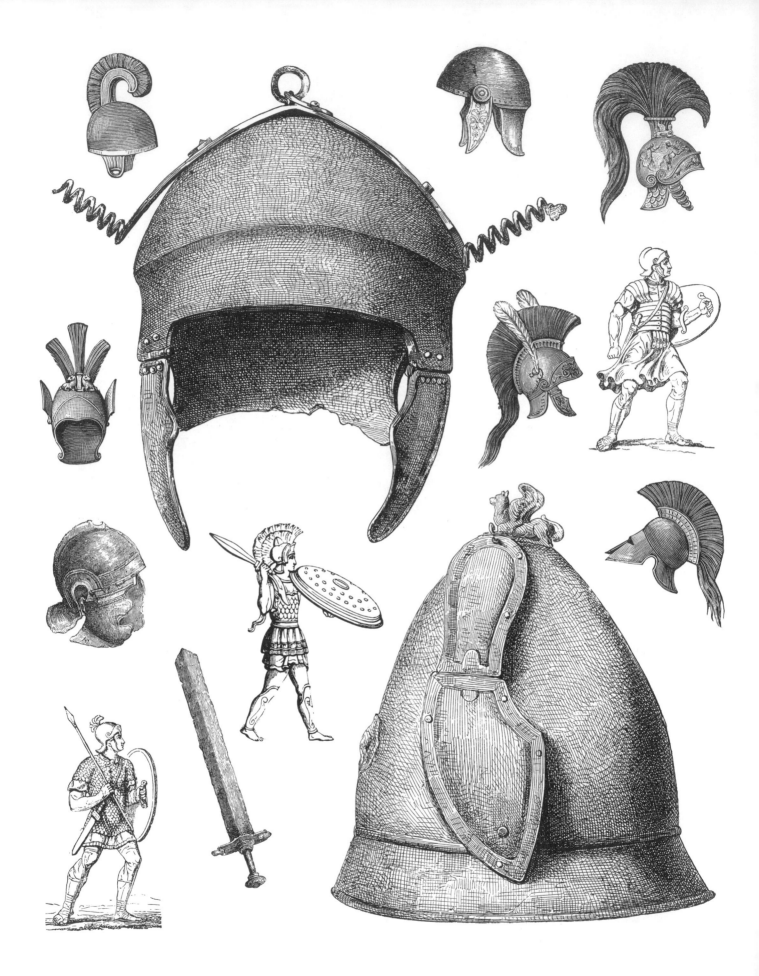

2　　　　　　　　　　Greek, Roman and Assyrian.

Greek and Roman.

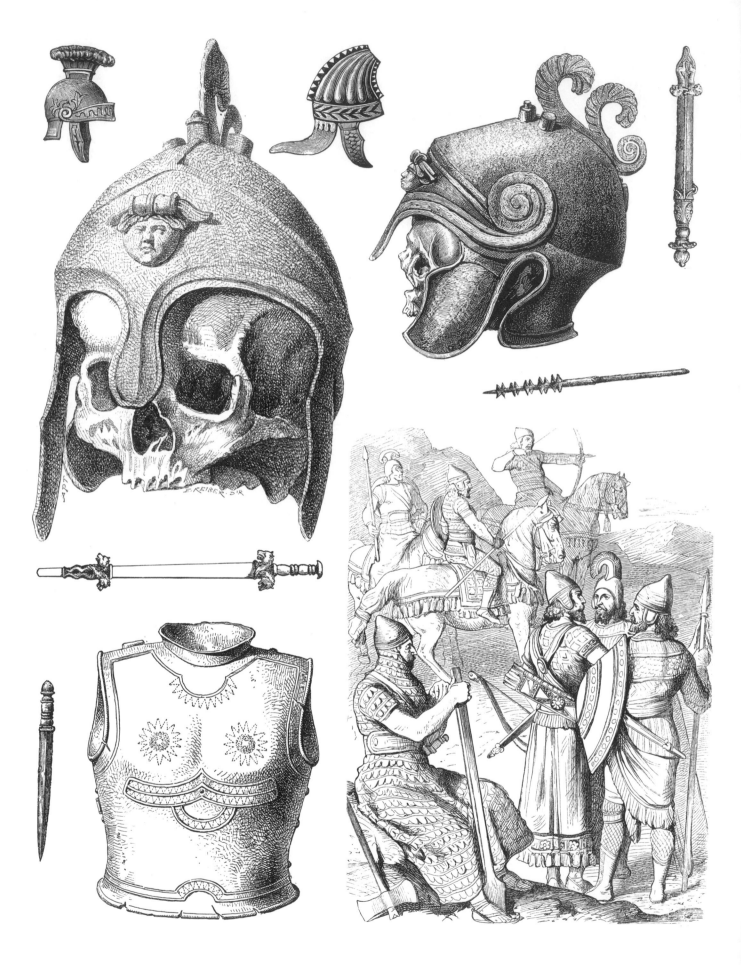

4   Assyrian, Greek, Etruscan, Roman and Gallic.

Gallic and Assyrian.

6 Gallic.

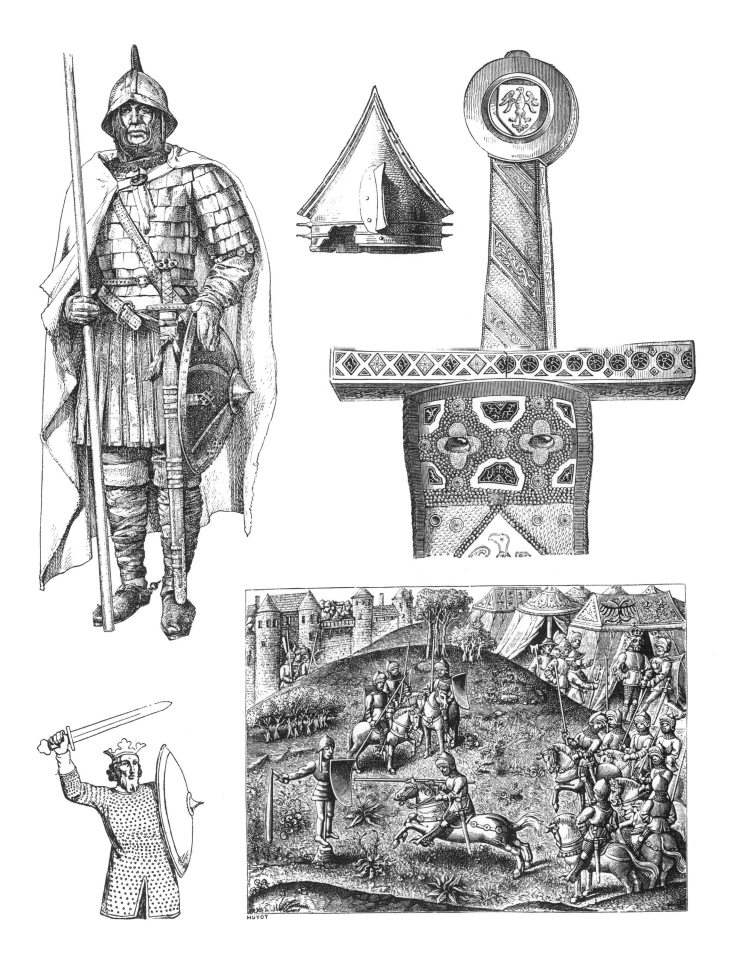

English *(8th-century)*, Frankish *(9th-century)*, unspecified *(9th- and 10th-century)* and Gallic.

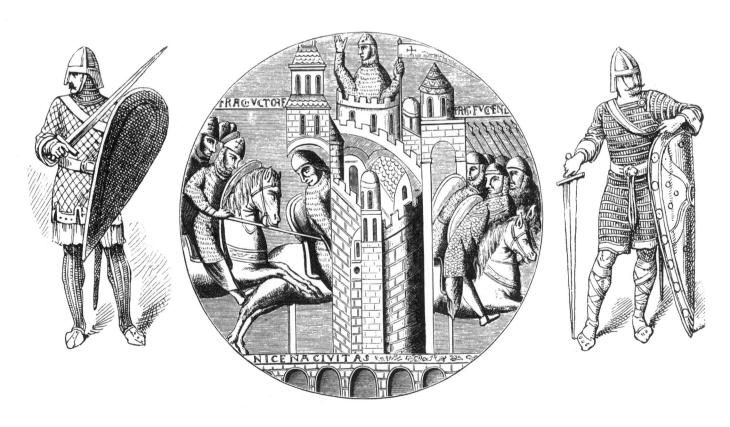

French *(11th-century)* and unspecified *(10th-century)*.

French *(11th-century)* and unspecified *(10th- and 11th-century).*

English, various periods.

English *(ca. 12th-century)*, French *(12th-century)* and unspecified.

12   German and unspecified *(12th-century)* and French *(12th- and 13th-century).*

French and English *(13th-century)* and unspecified.

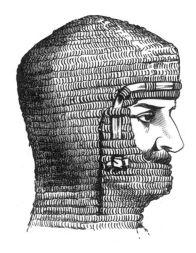

French *(13th-century).*

French *(13th-century).*

16   English, French and German (*13th-century*).

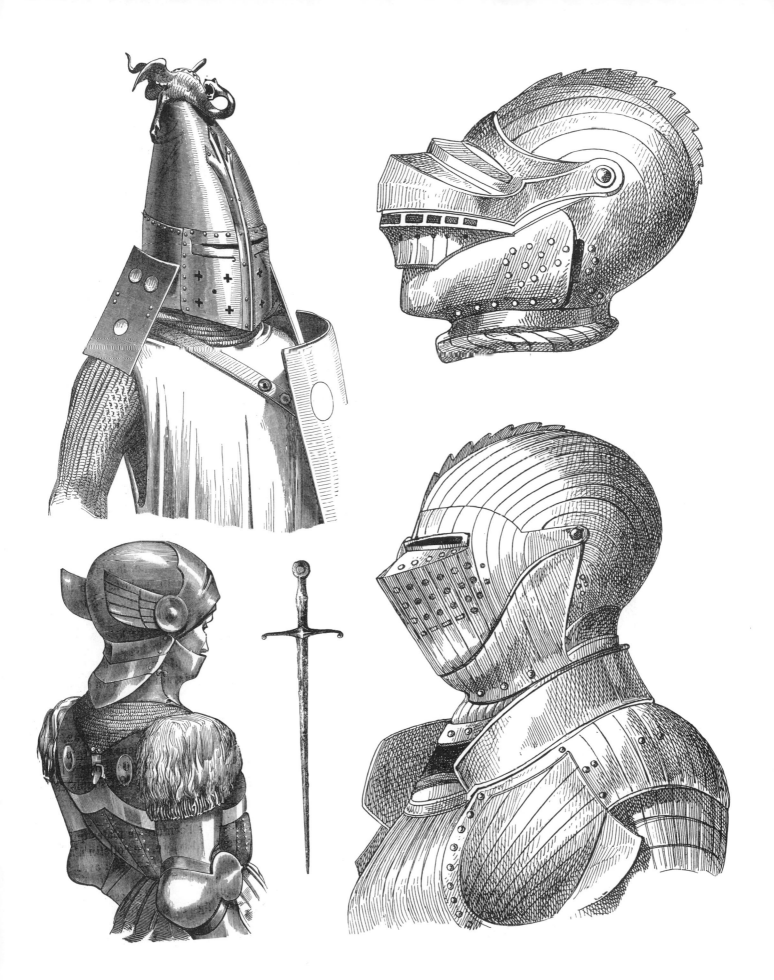

French *(13th- and 14th-century)*.

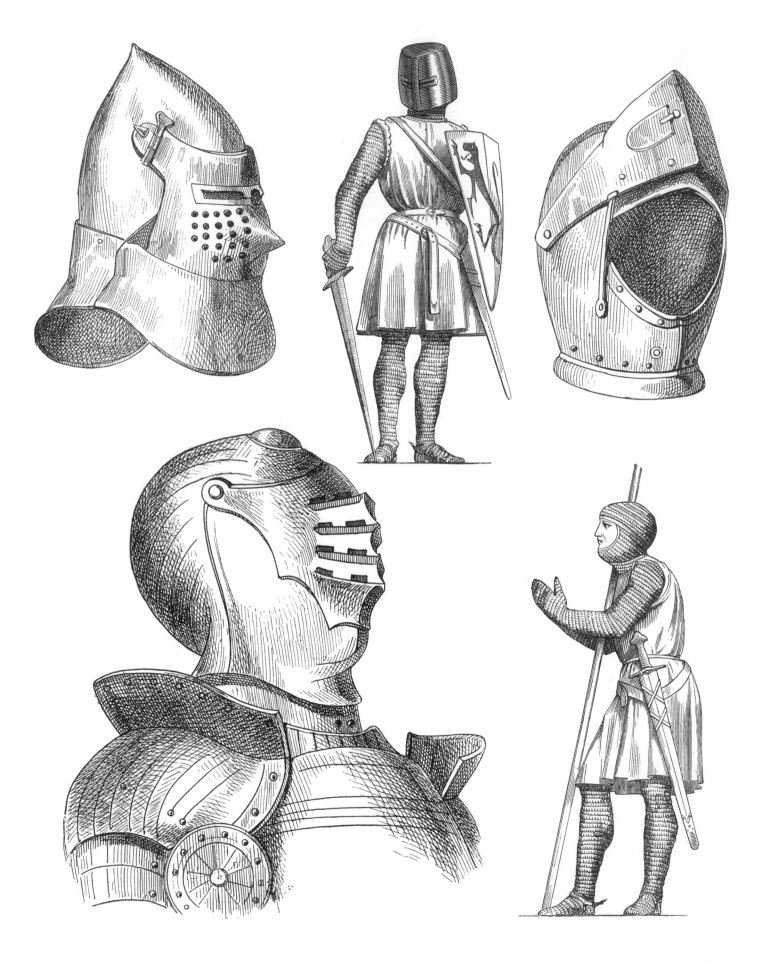

French *(13th- and 14th-century)*.

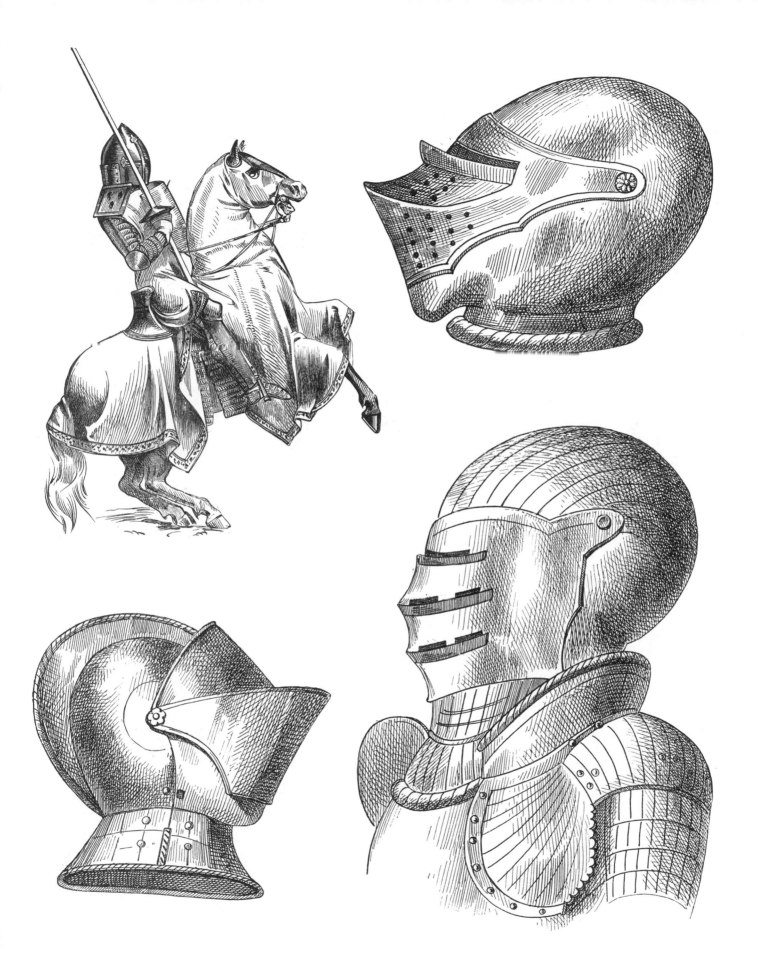

French *(13th- and 14th-century).*

20   French and English *(14th-century).*

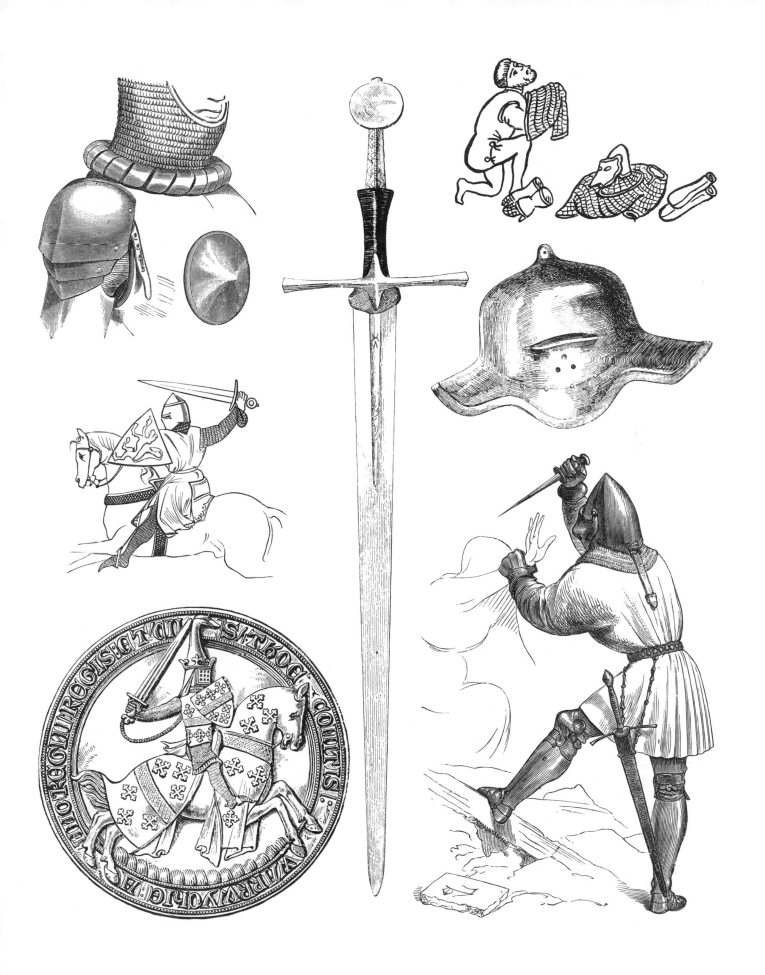

French, English and German *(14th-century)*.

French and English *(14th-century)*

English, French and Spanish *(14th-century)*.

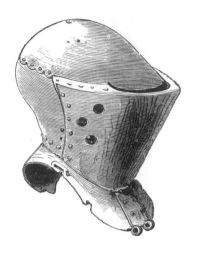

French and unspecified *(14th-century)*.

French and English *(14th-century)*.

French (*14th-century*) and unspecified.

French and German *(14th-century)*.

French and German (*14th-century*).

French, Italian, English and German (*14th-century*).

30   German, Swiss, Spanish, French and unspecified *(15th-century)*.

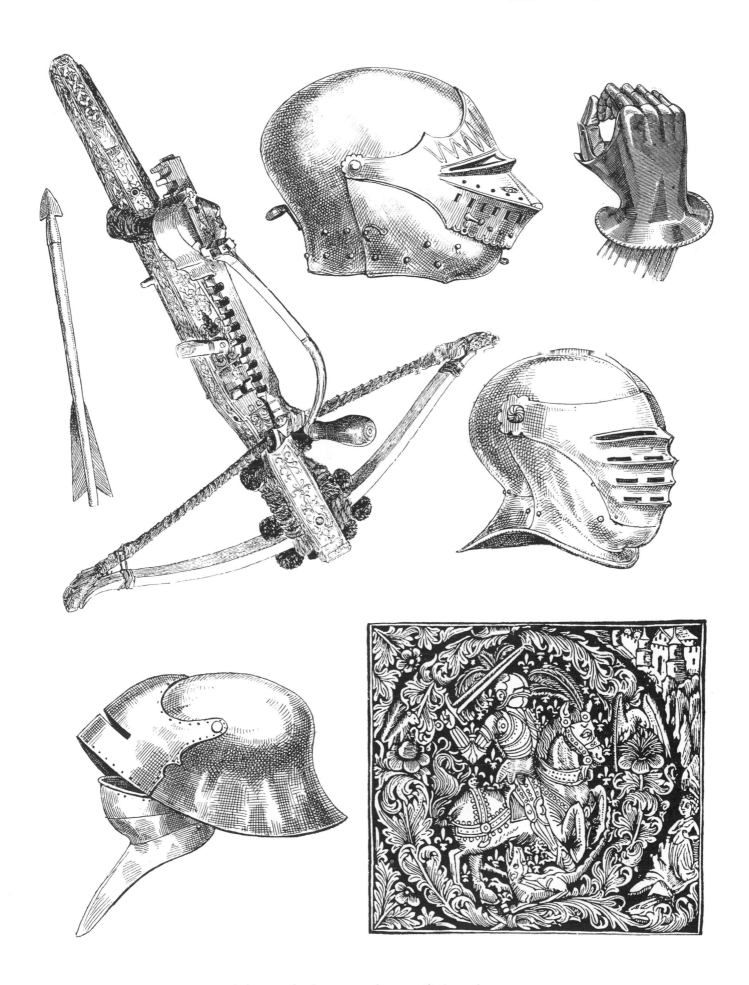

English, French, German and unspecified *(15th-century)*.

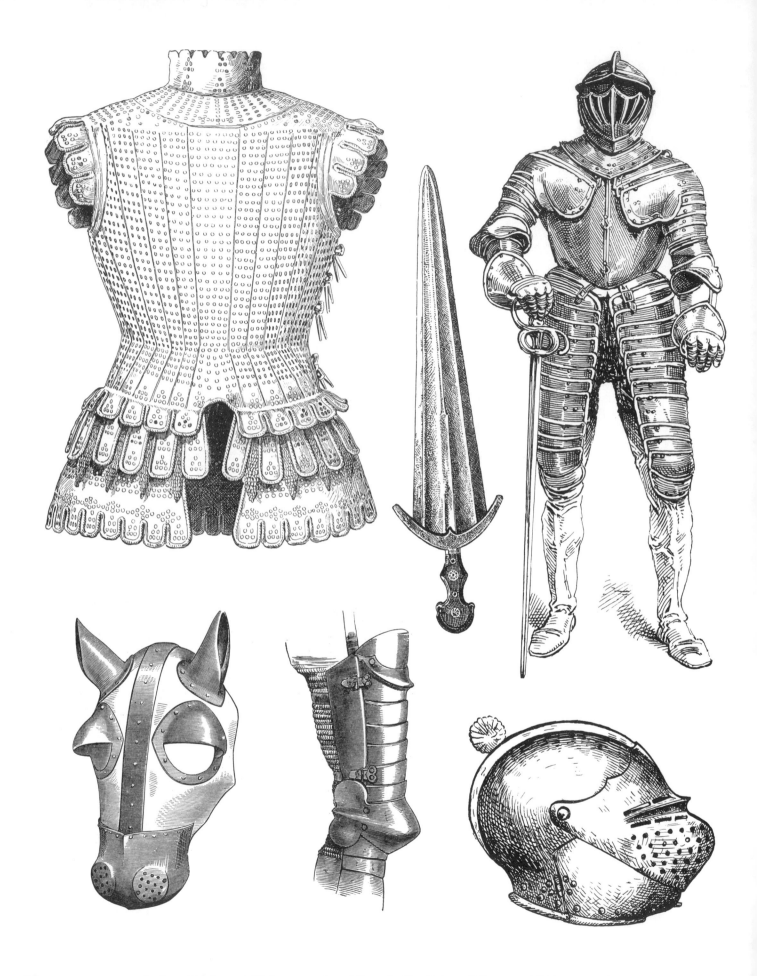

Italian *(14th- and 15th-century)* and French, English and German *(15th-century)*.

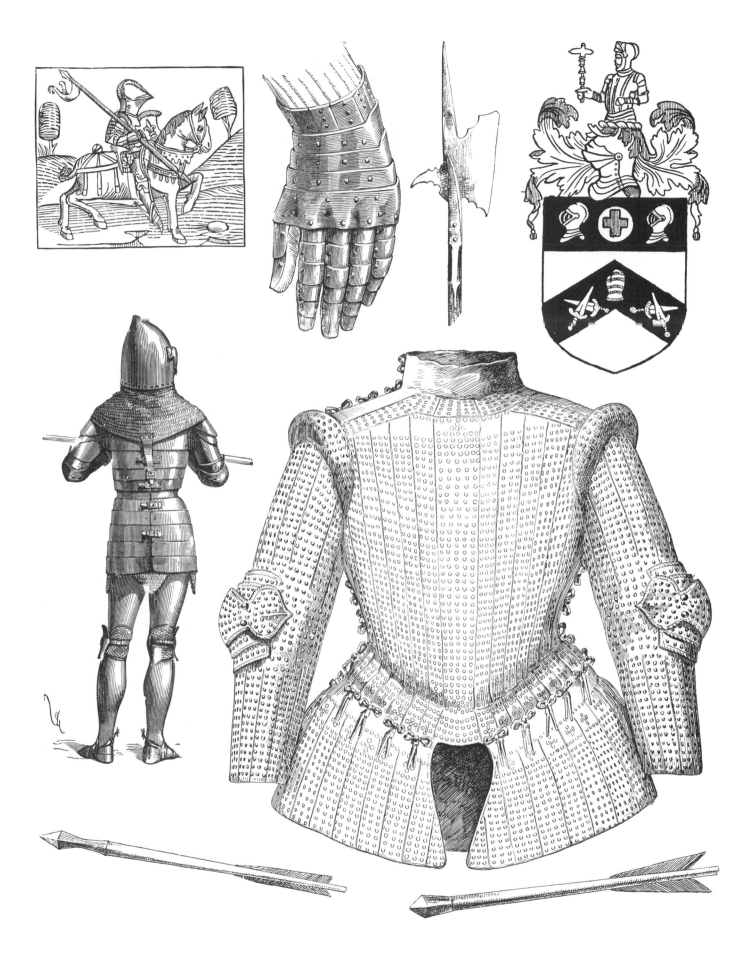

Italian *(14th- and 15th-century)* and English, French, Swiss and unspecified *(15th-century)*.   33

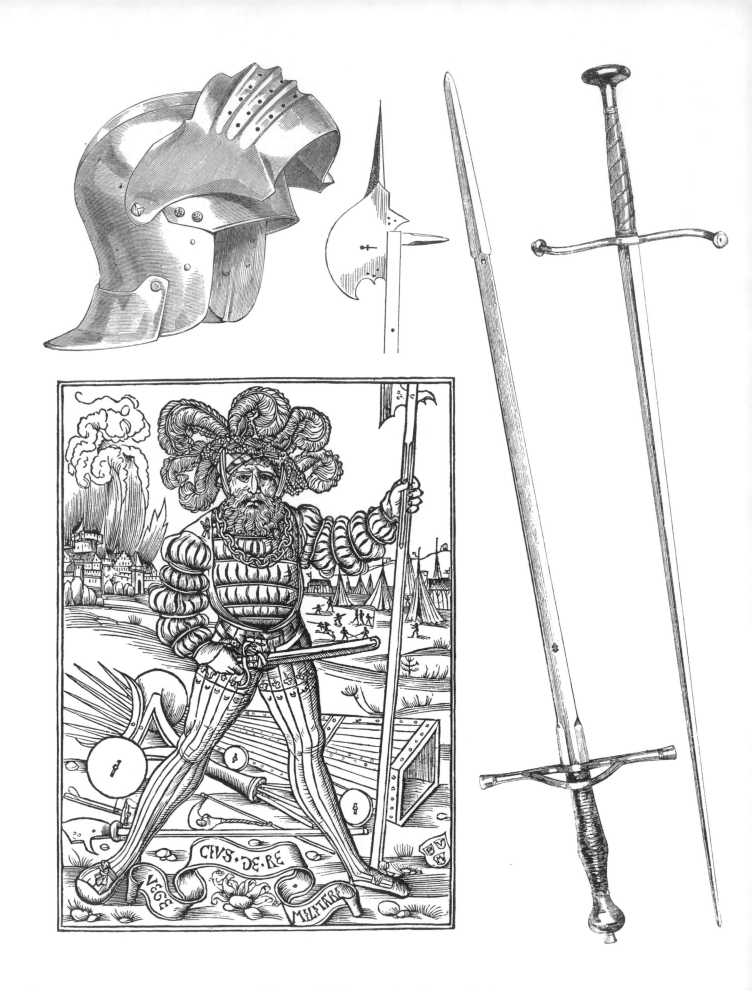

German *(15th-century)* and unspecified.

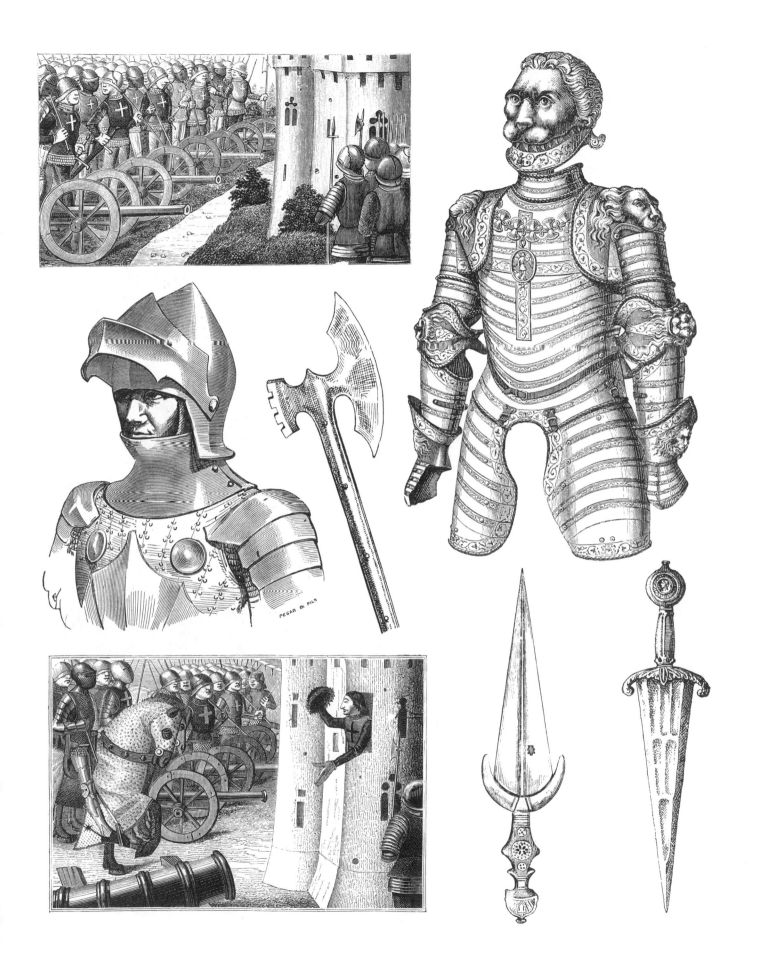

French, German and Italian (*15th-century*).

35

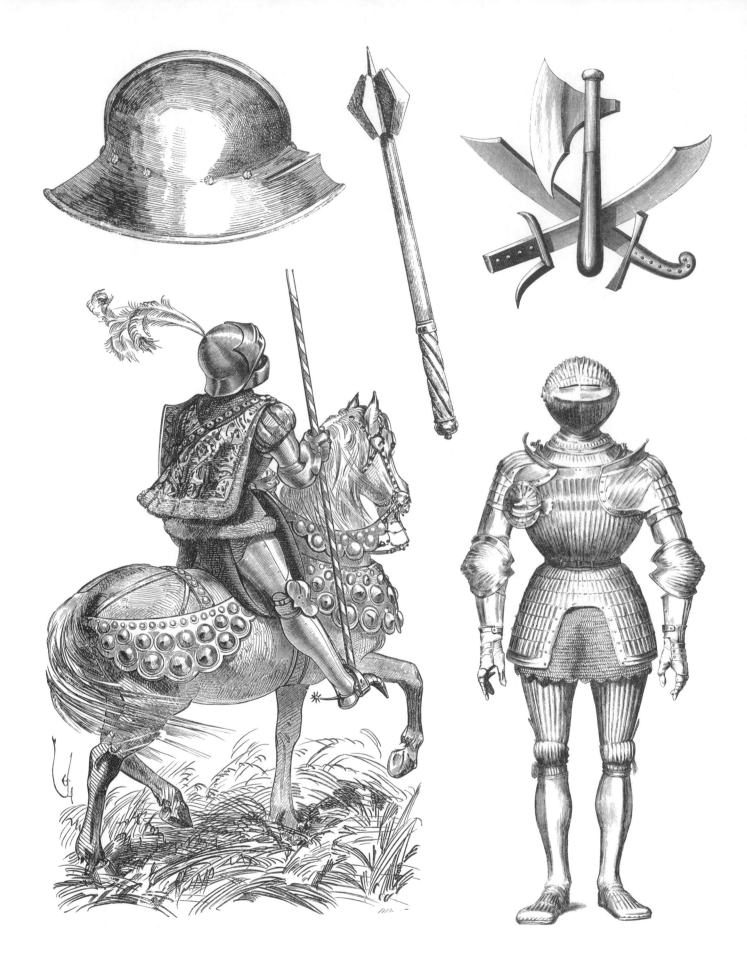

36   German, English, French and unspecified *(15th-century)*.

French, German and unspecified *(15th-century)*.

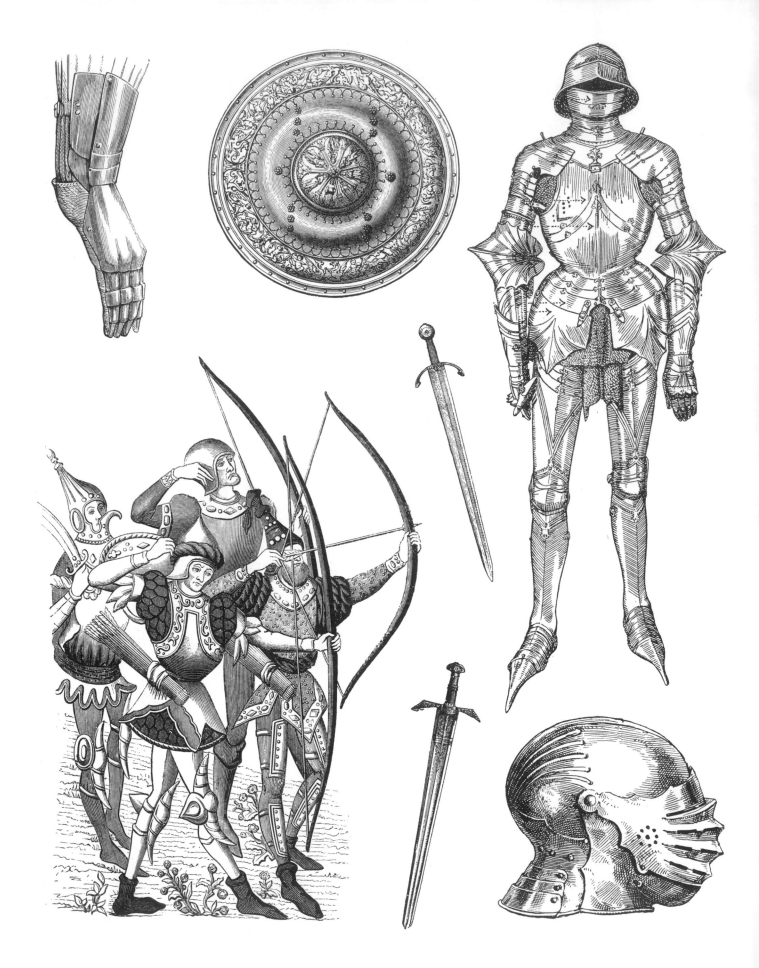

French, German and Spanish *(15th-century).*

French, Italian, Spanish and German *(15th-century)*.

39

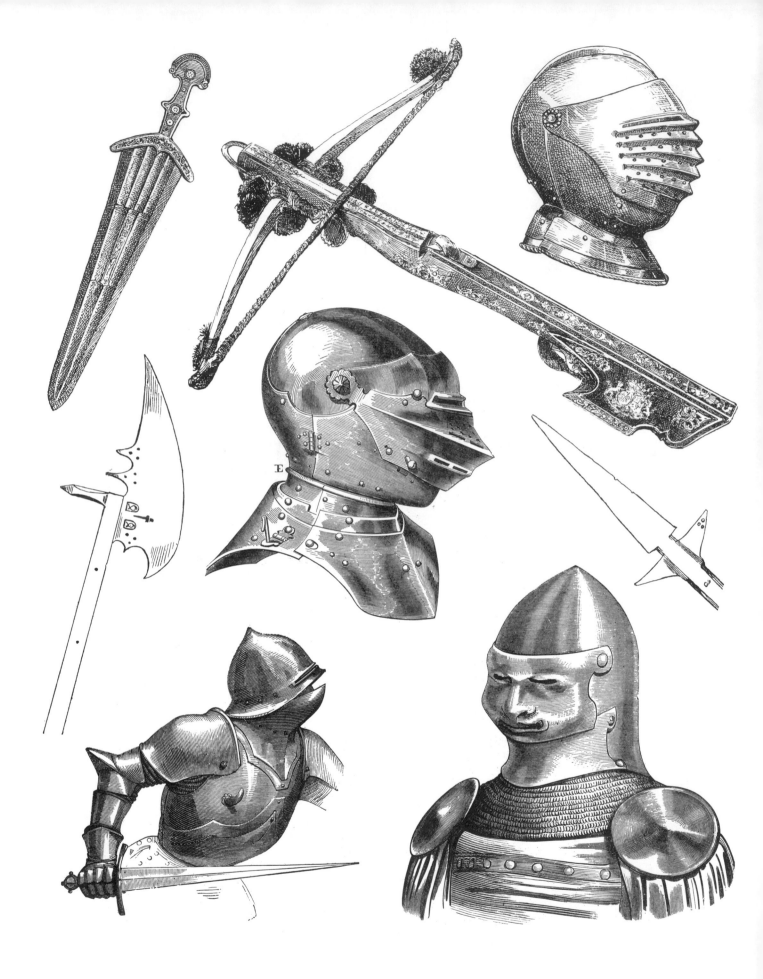

40   French, Italian, English, German and unspecified *(15th-century)*.

Italian, English, French and unspecified *(15th-century)*.

42   French, English and unspecified *(15th-century)*.

French, English, German and Spanish *(15th-century)*.

43

44   French and German *(15th-century)*.

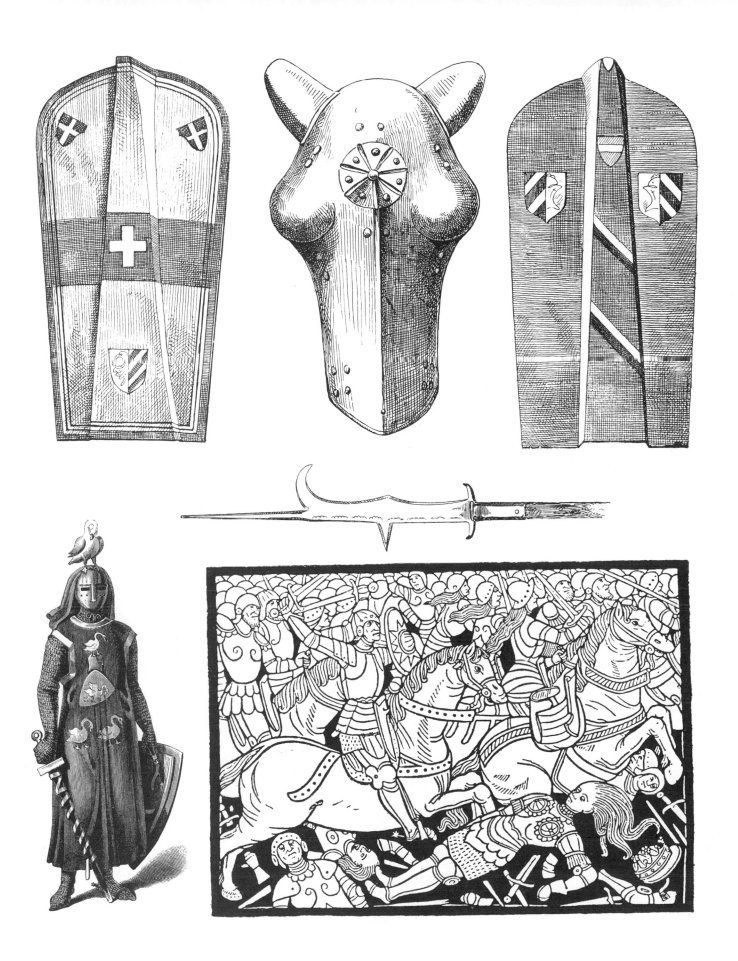

German, French and unspecified *(15th-century).*

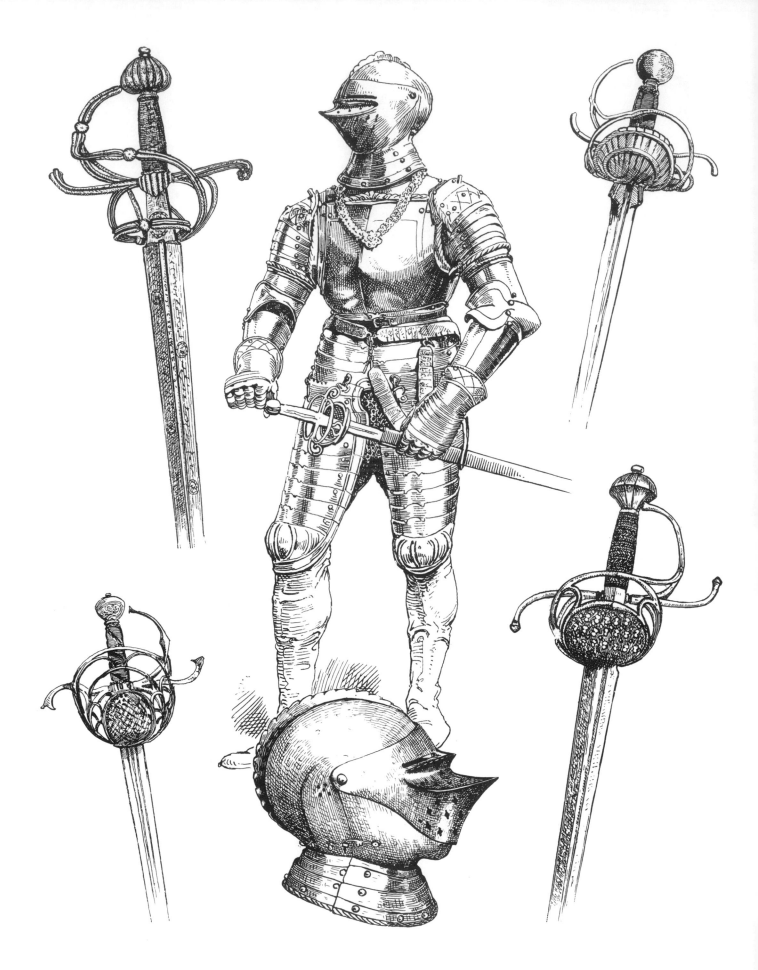

English *(16th-century)*.

English and Italian *(16th-century).*

48   Italian, Spanish, Indian, Portuguese and German *(16th-century)*.

Italian, German and unspecified *(16th-century)*.

49

50   English, Spanish and unspecified *(16th-century)*.

English, French and German *(16th-century)*.

51

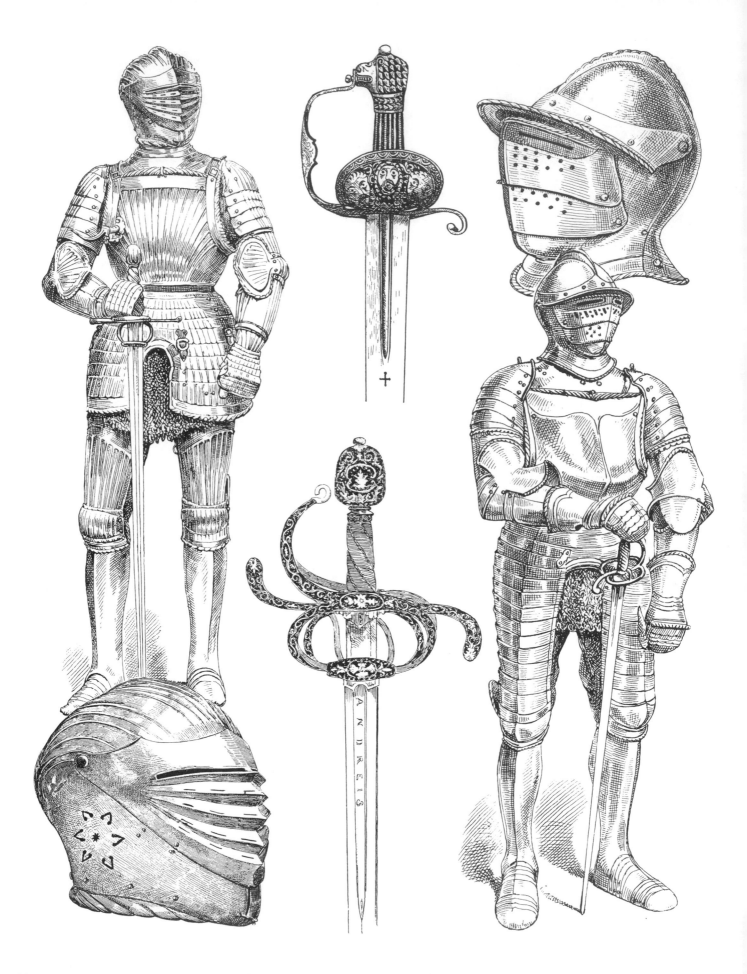

German, English and Italian *(16th-century)*.

Italian, English and German *(16th-century)*.

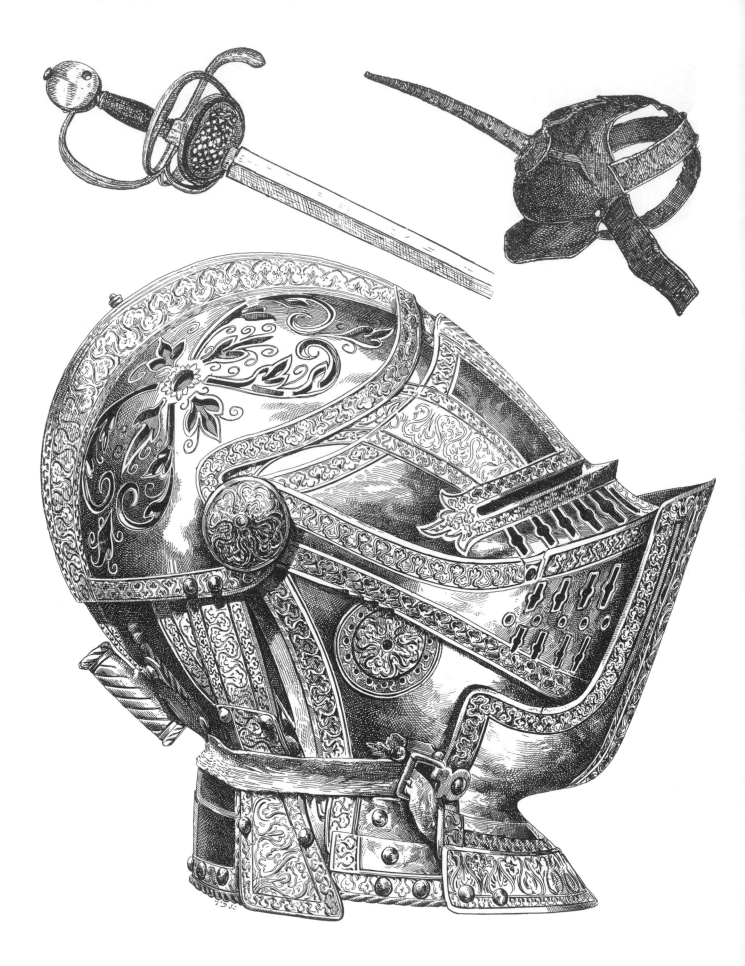

54 German and English (*16th-century*).

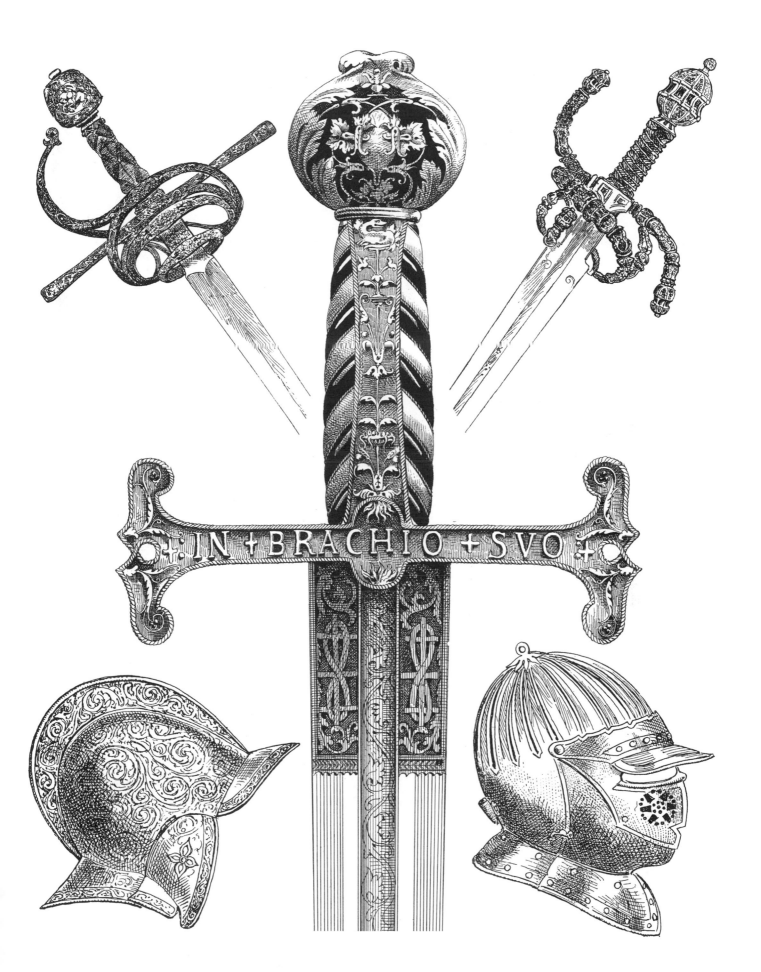

Italian, Italo-Spanish and English *(16th-century)*.

German and unspecified *(16th-century)*.

German and English *(16th-century).*

English, Indian and German *(16th-century)*.

German, Italian, French and unspecified *(16th-century)*.

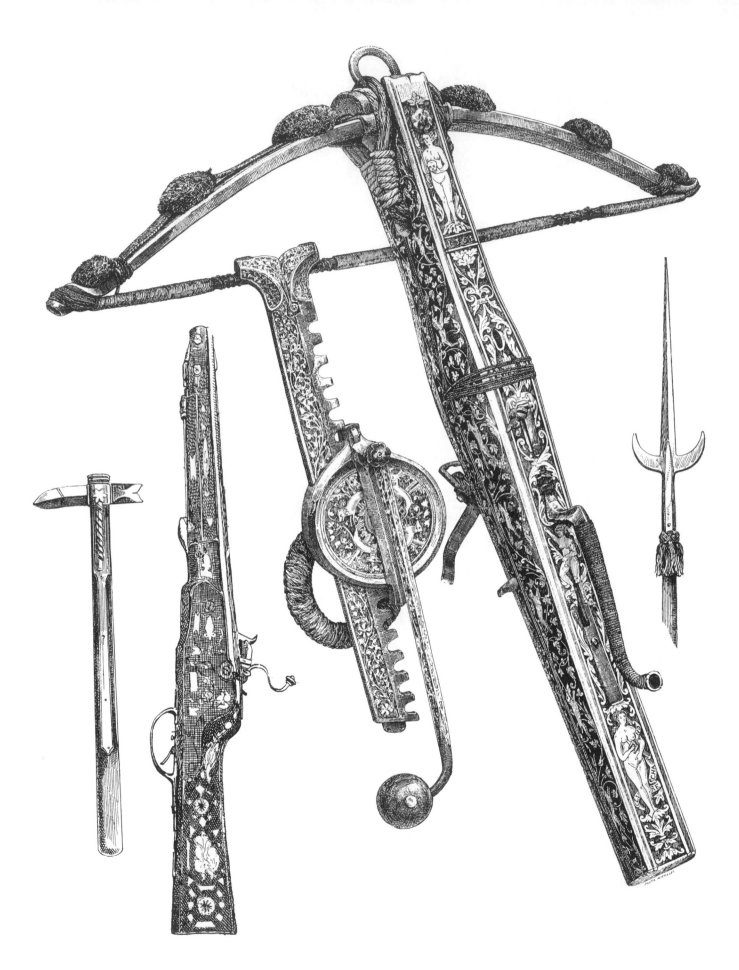

German and unspecified *(16th-century)*.

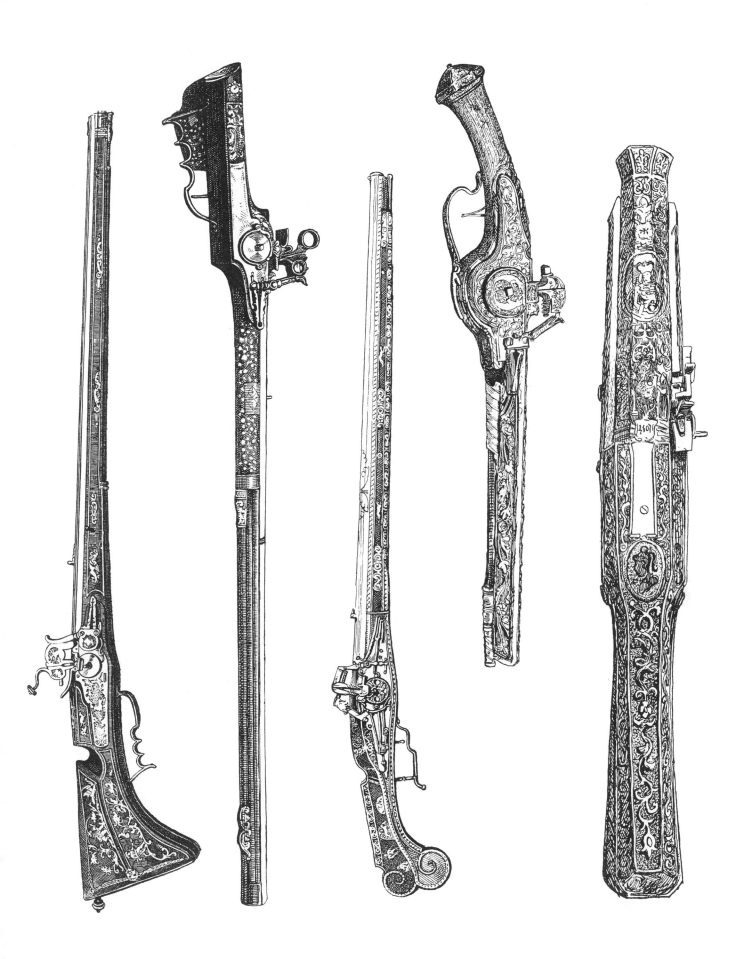

English and unspecified *(16th-century)*.

62   English and German *(16th-century).*

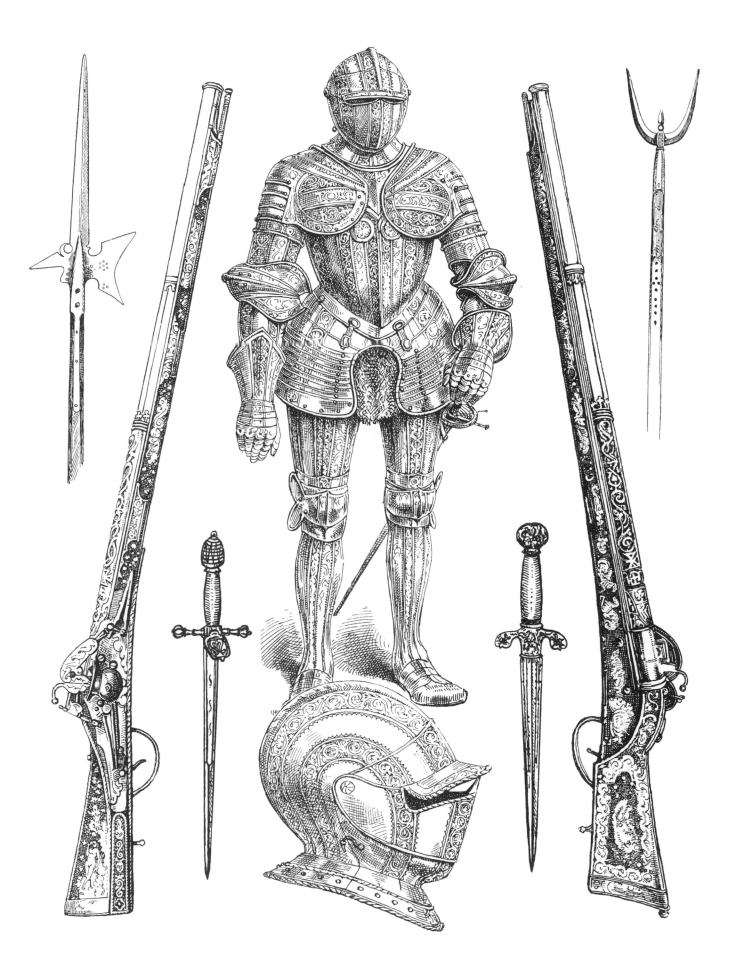

English, Swiss, Spanish and unspecified *(16th-century)*.

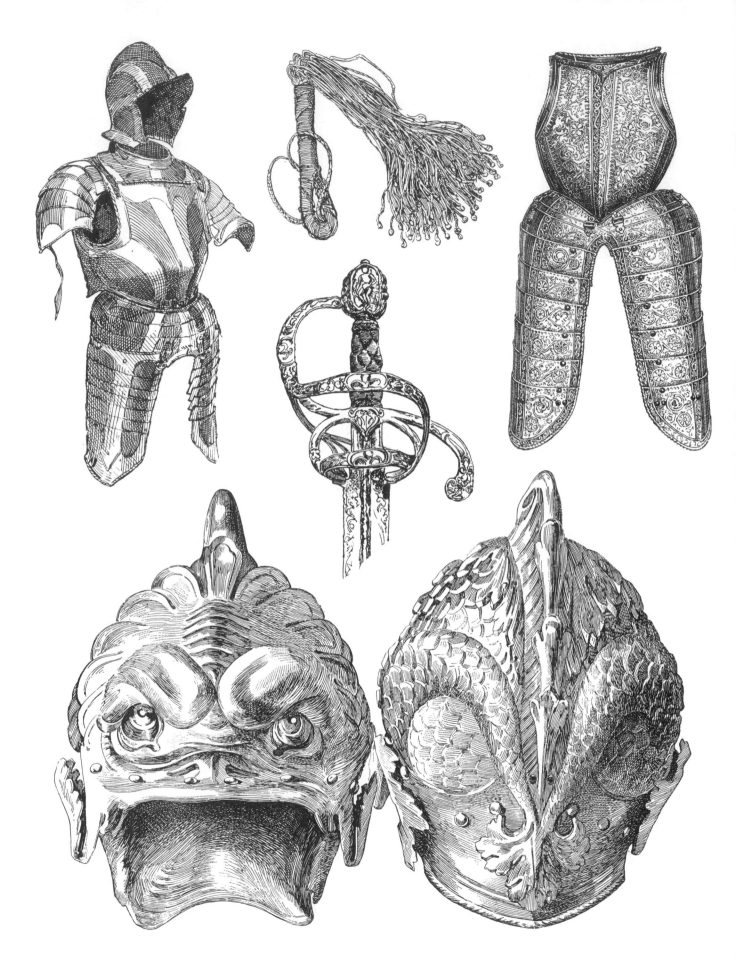

English, German, Russian and Italian *(16th-century)*.

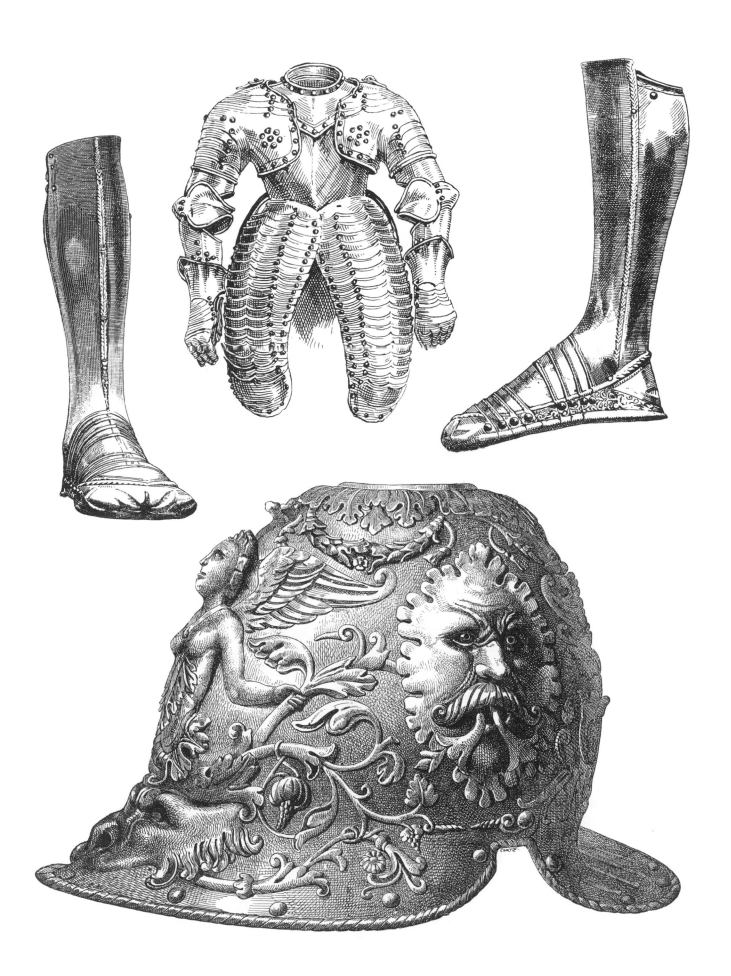

English, German and unspecified *(16th-century)*.

German, English and Italian *(16th-century)*.

Spanish, French, English and unspecified *(16th-century)*.

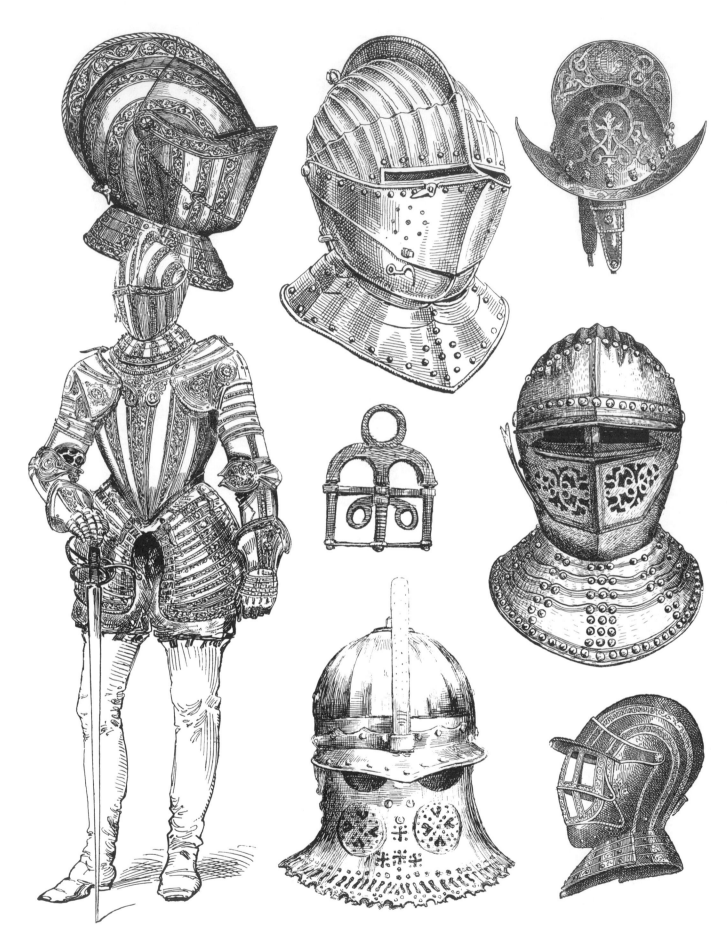

Spanish, English, French and Polish *(16th-century)*.

Polish and unspecified *(16th-century)*.

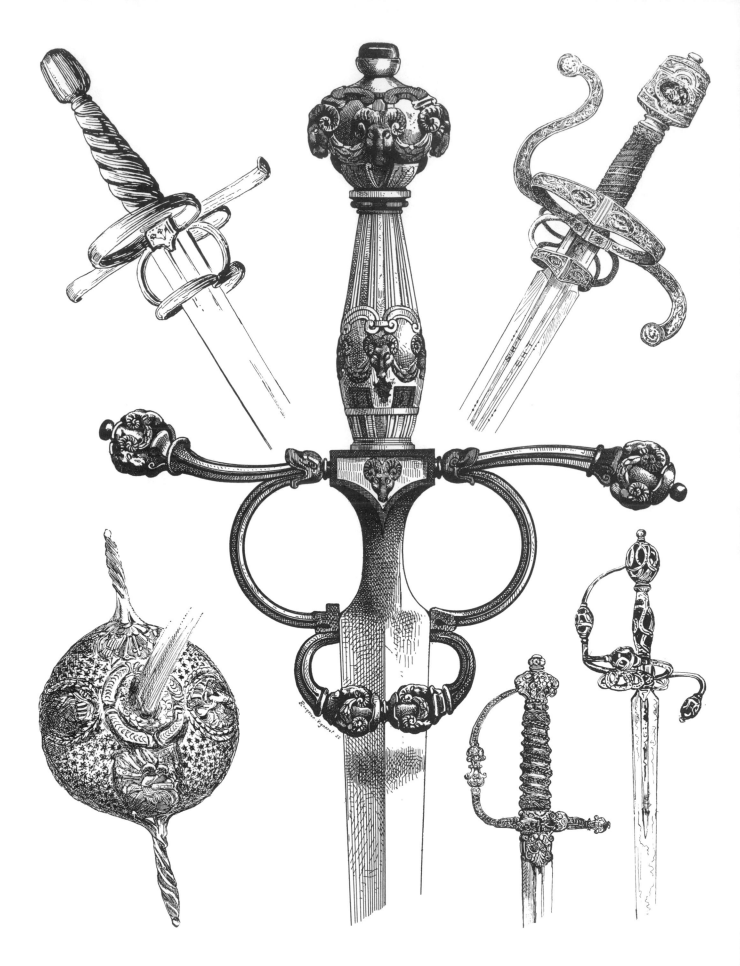

English, French, Italian, Spanish and unspecified *(16th-century)*.

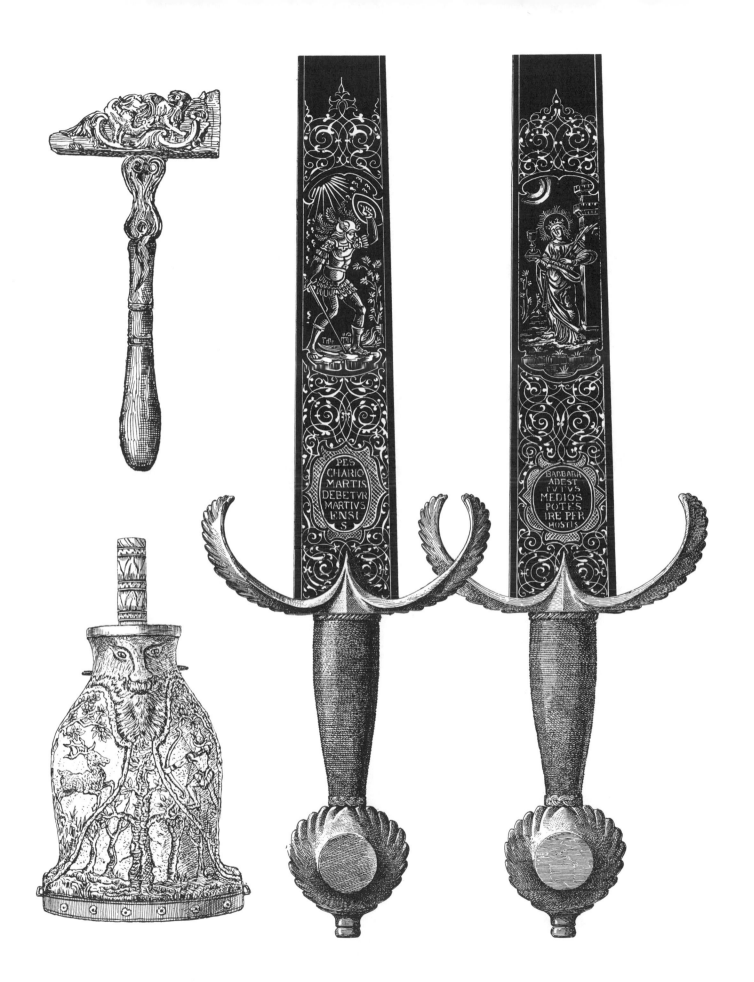

Italian and German *(16th-century)*.

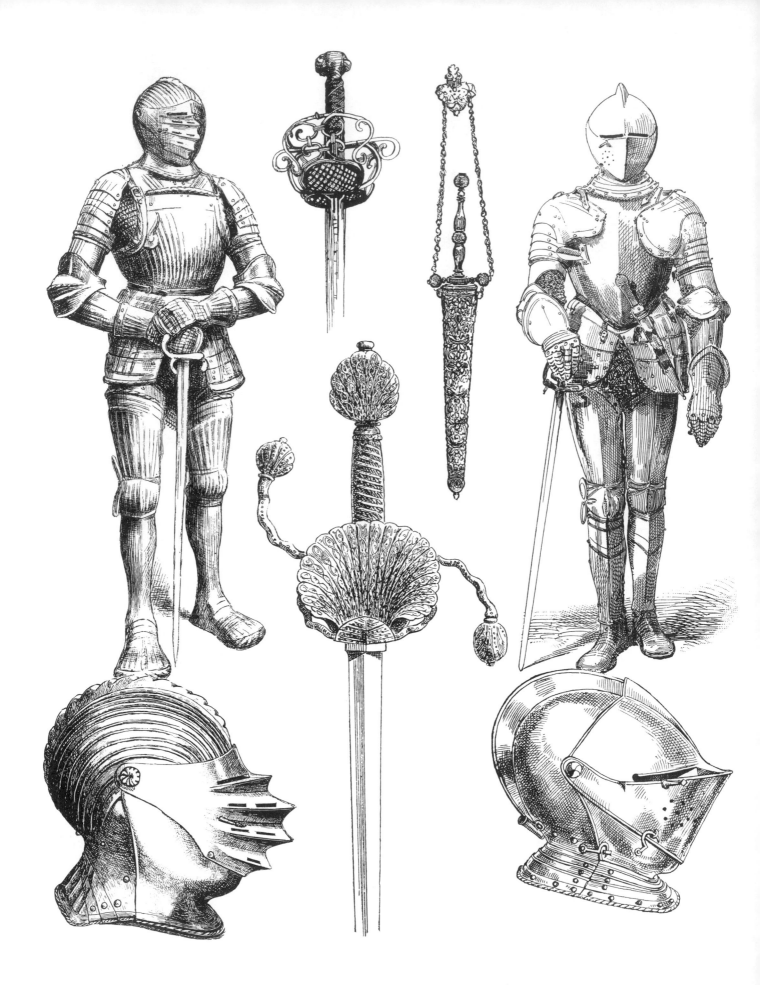

German, English, Italian and unspecified *(16th-century)*.

German, English, Italian and French *(16th-century)*.

74   Flemish, English, Burmese and Italian *(16th-century)*.

German, Italian, English and French *(16th-century)*.

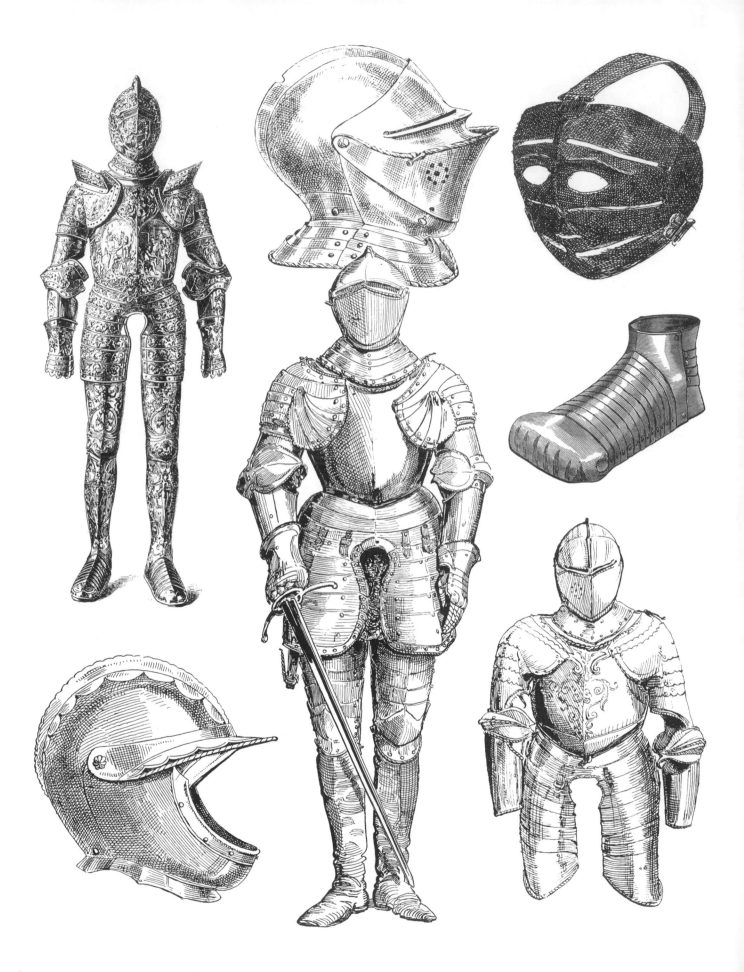

French, German, English and unspecified *(16th-century)*.

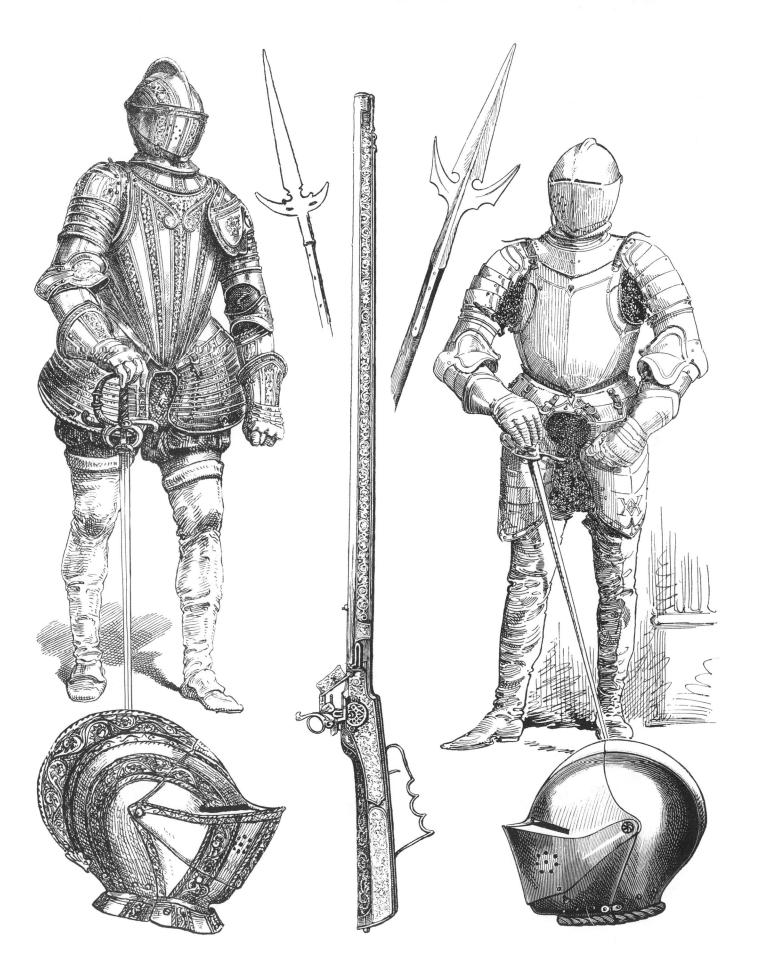

Spanish, English, Italian, German and unspecified (16th-century).

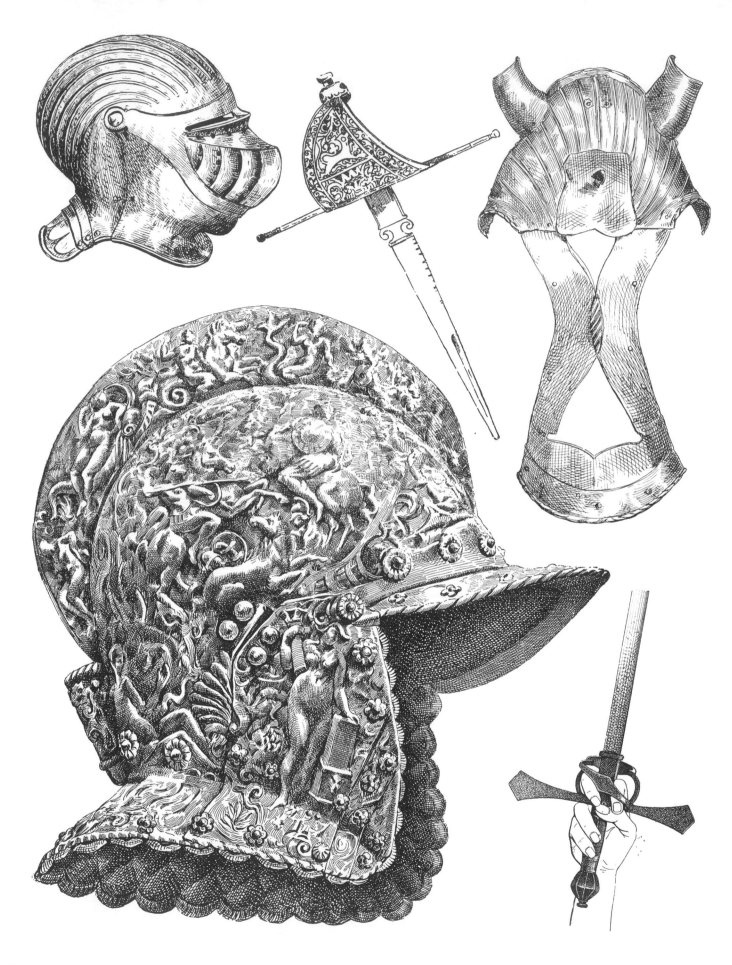

German, English and unspecified *(16th-century)*.

English, French, Spanish and German *(16th-century)*.

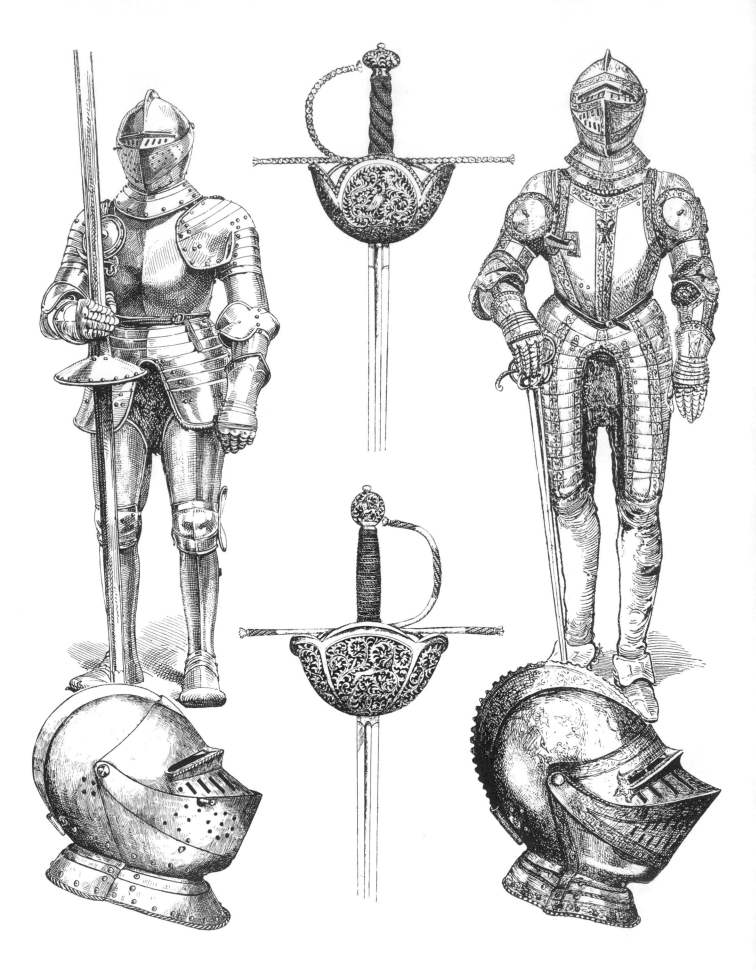

English, Italian and German *(16th-century)*.

Spanish and Italian *(16th-century)*.

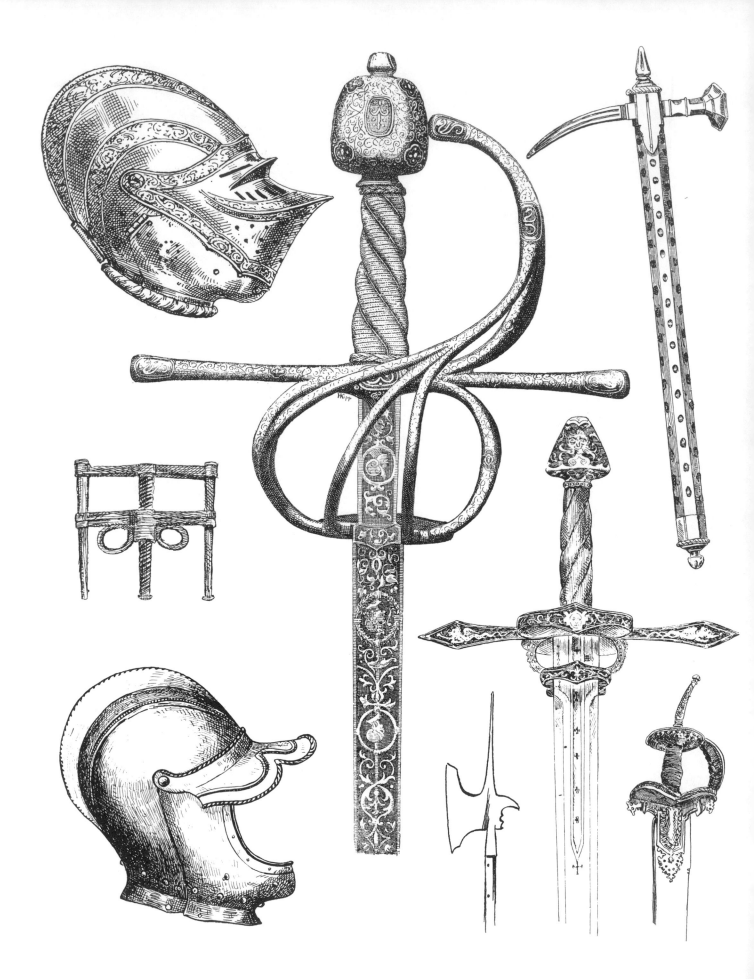

English, Italian, Swiss and Indian *(16th-century)*.

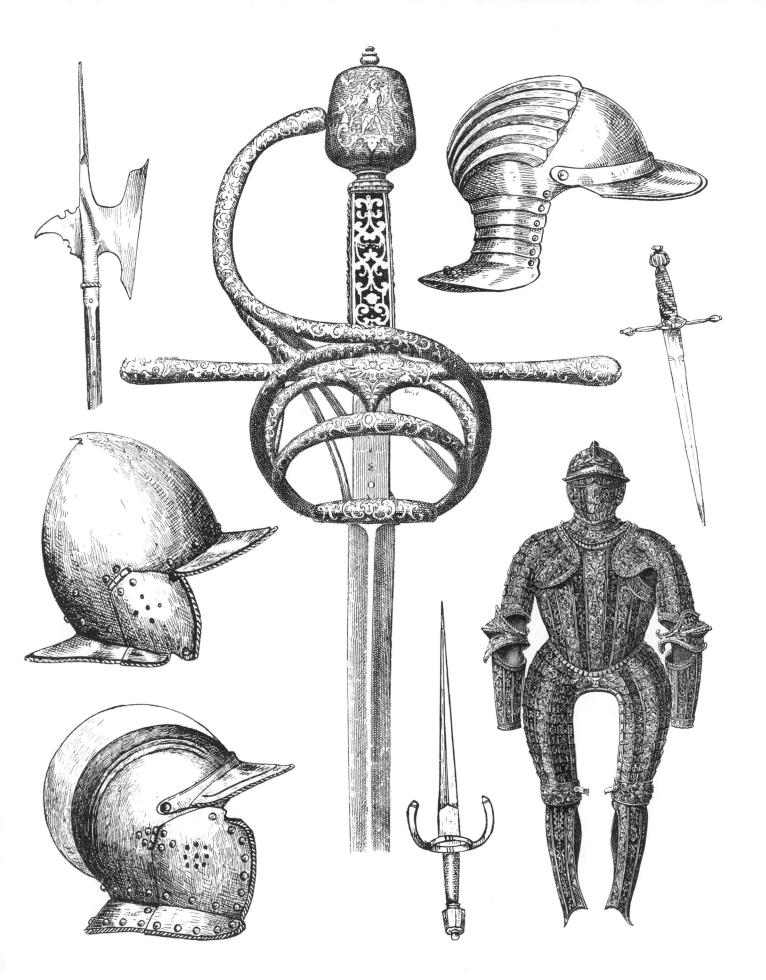

English, French, German and unspecified *(16th-century)*.

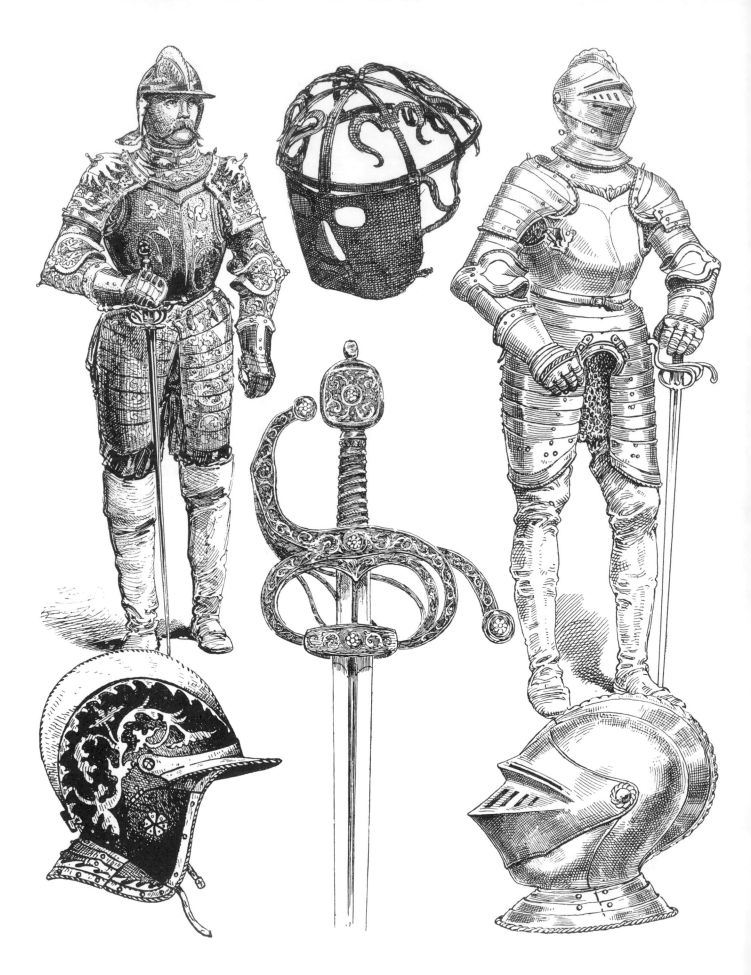

Italian, German and unspecified *(16th-century)*.

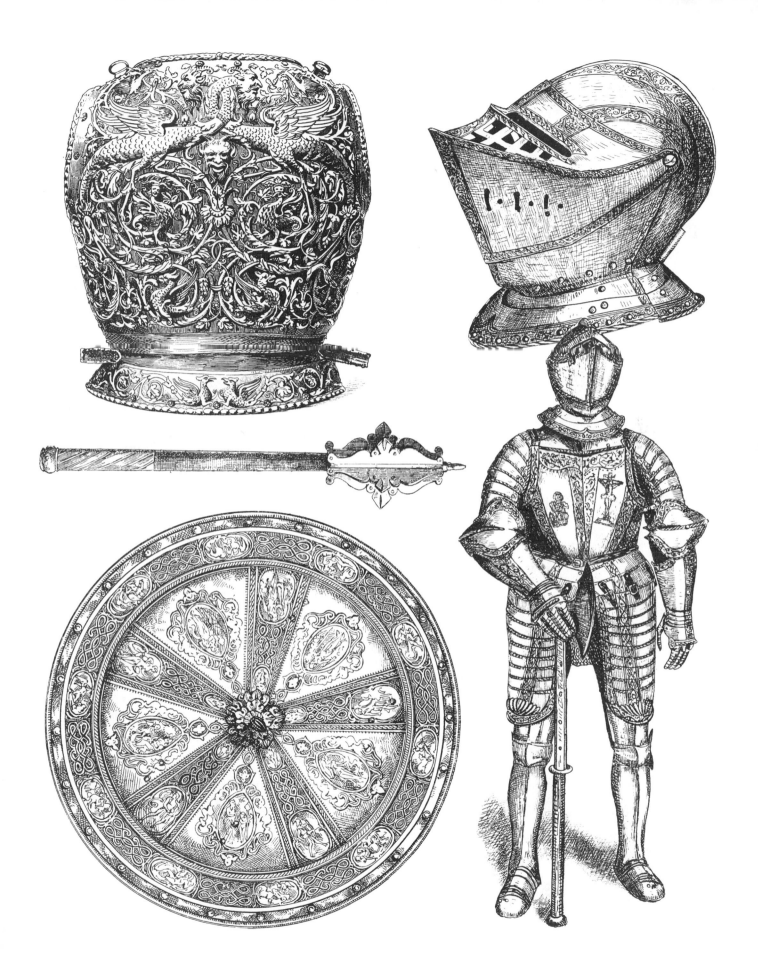

English, French, Italian and German *(16th-century).*

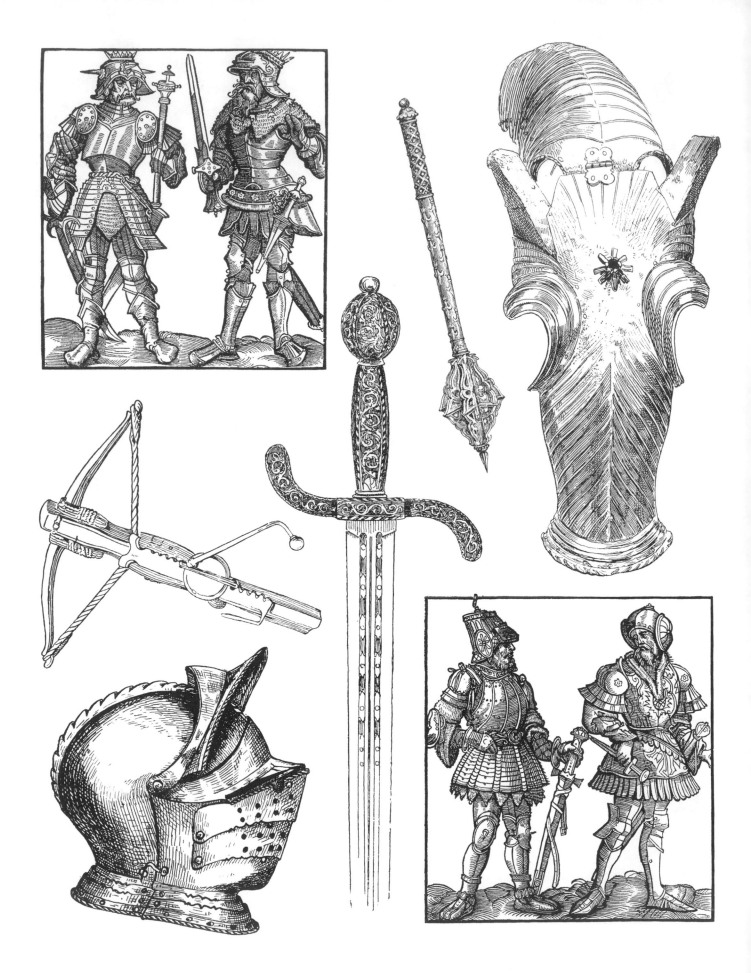

German, English, Italian, Spanish and unspecified *(16th-century)*.

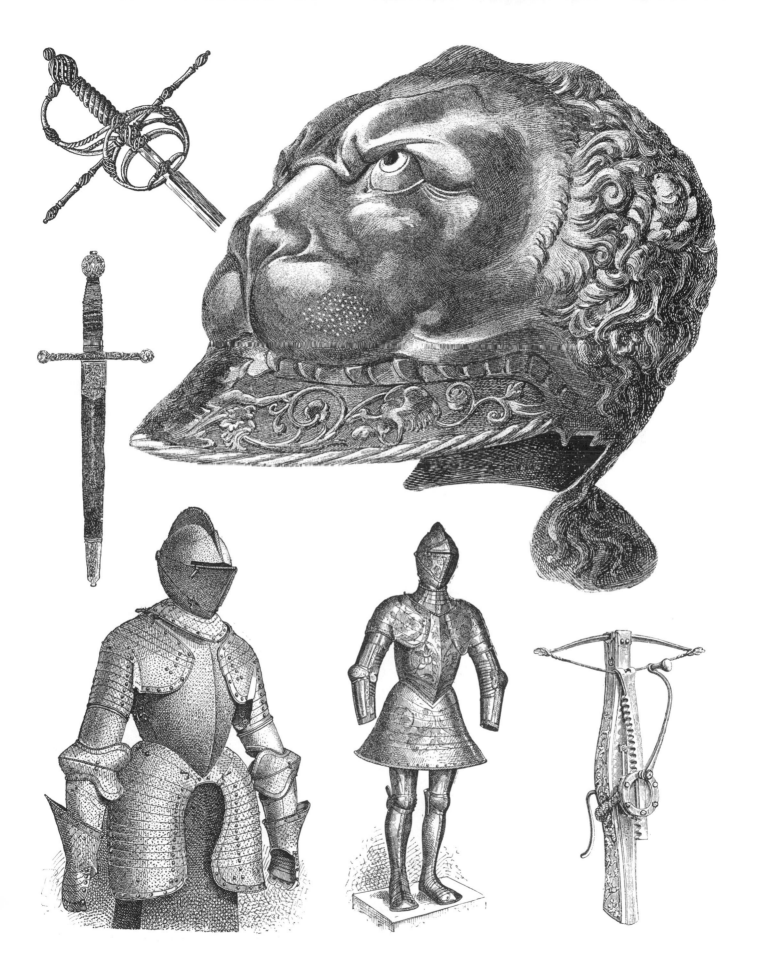

Italian, English, Spanish and unspecified *(16th-century)*.

German, Spanish and Italian *(16th-century).*

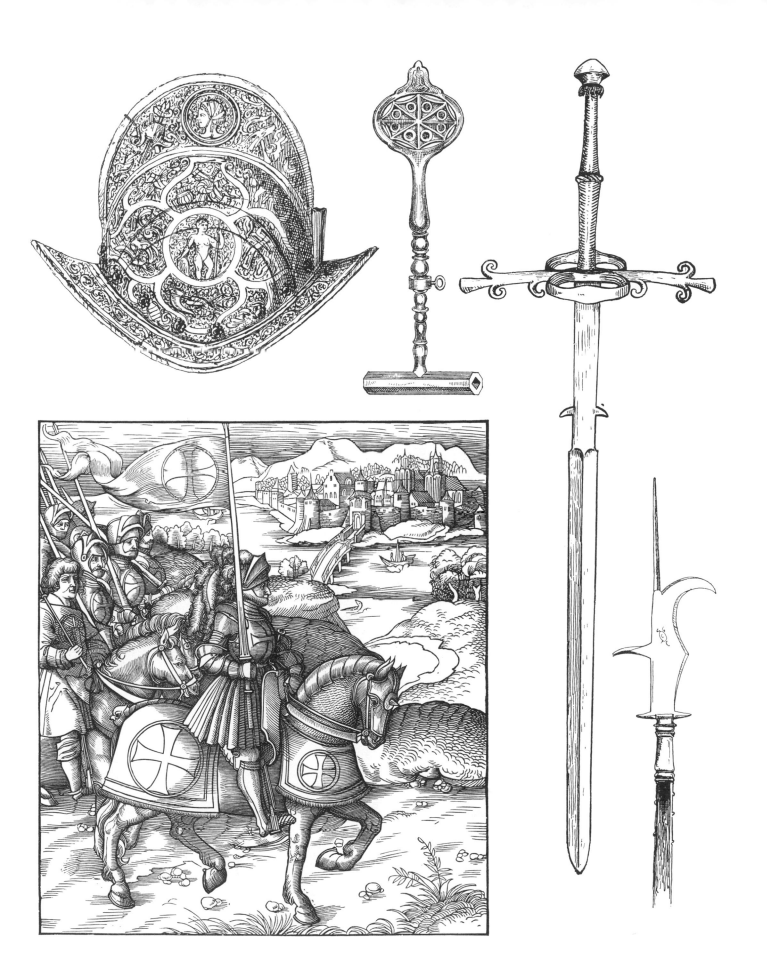

Italian, Swiss, German and unspecified *(16th-century)*.

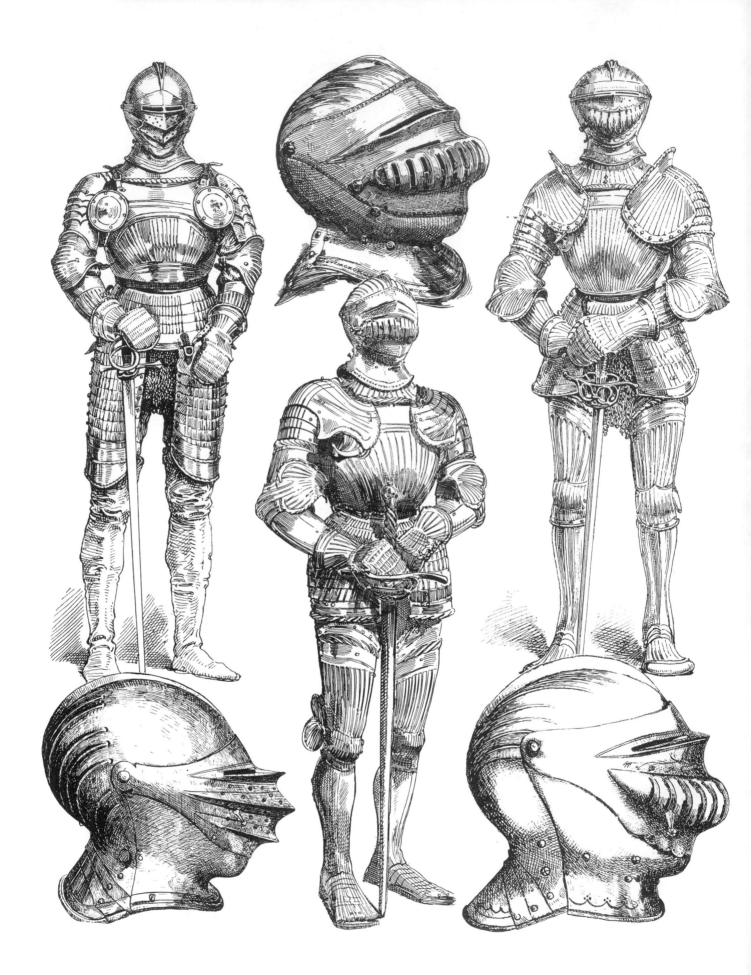

German *(16th-century)*.

French, English and German *(16th-century)*.

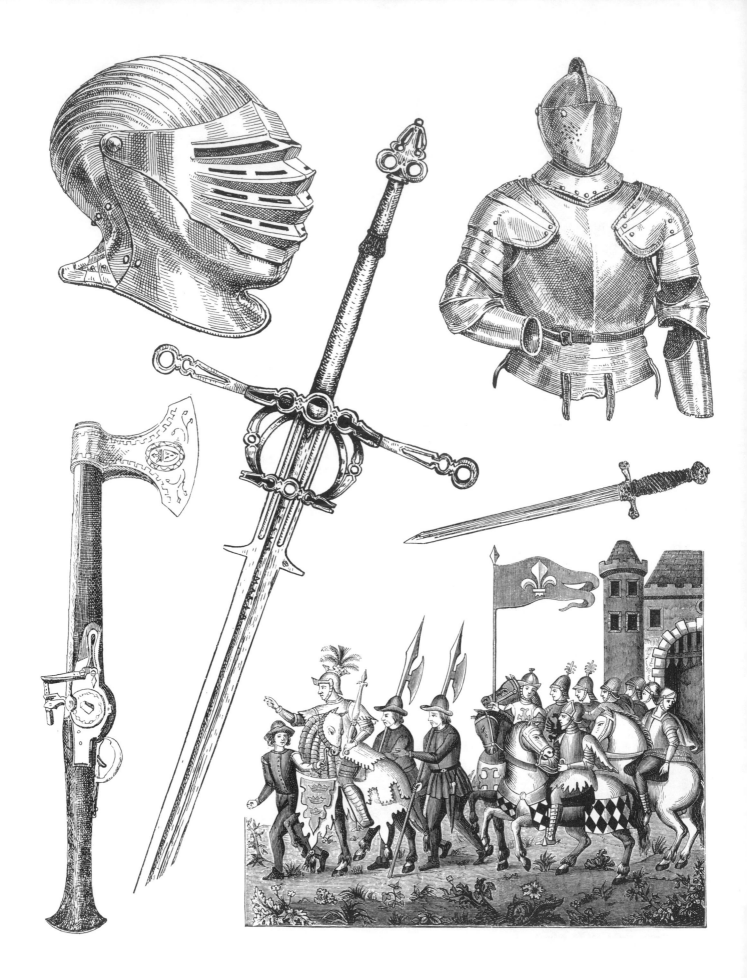

English, Spanish, French and unspecified *(16th-century)*.

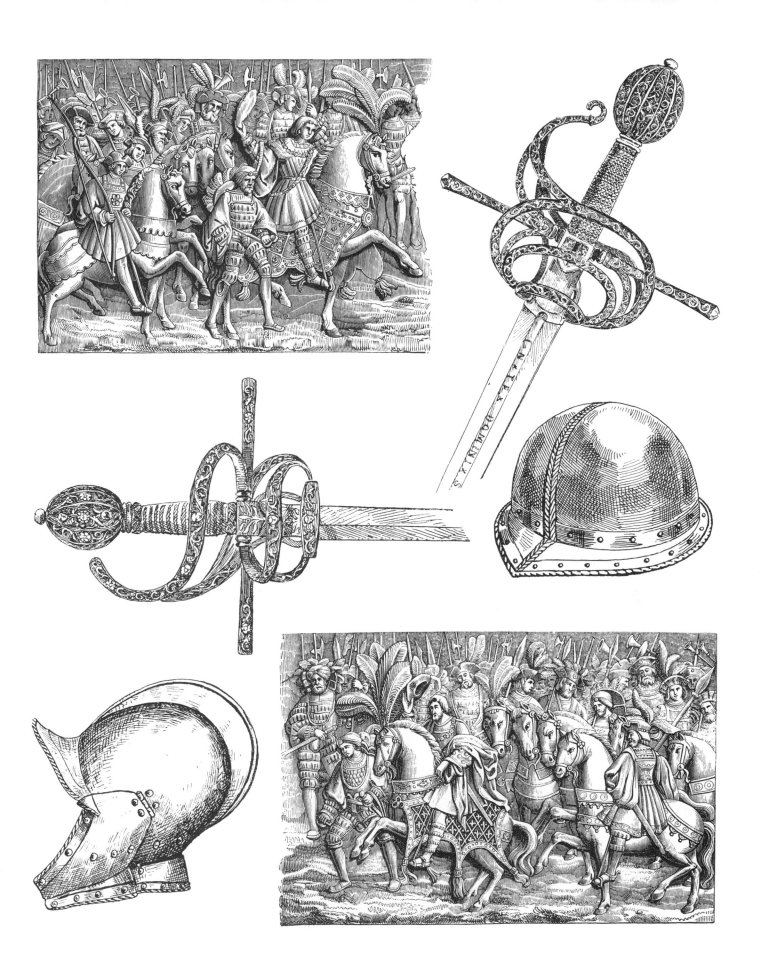

French, Italian, English and unspecified *(16th-century)*.

English, Italian, French and unspecified *(16th-century)*.

English *(16th- and 17th-century)* and Italian *(16th-century)*.

English, Spanish, French and unspecified *(16th- and 17th-century)*.

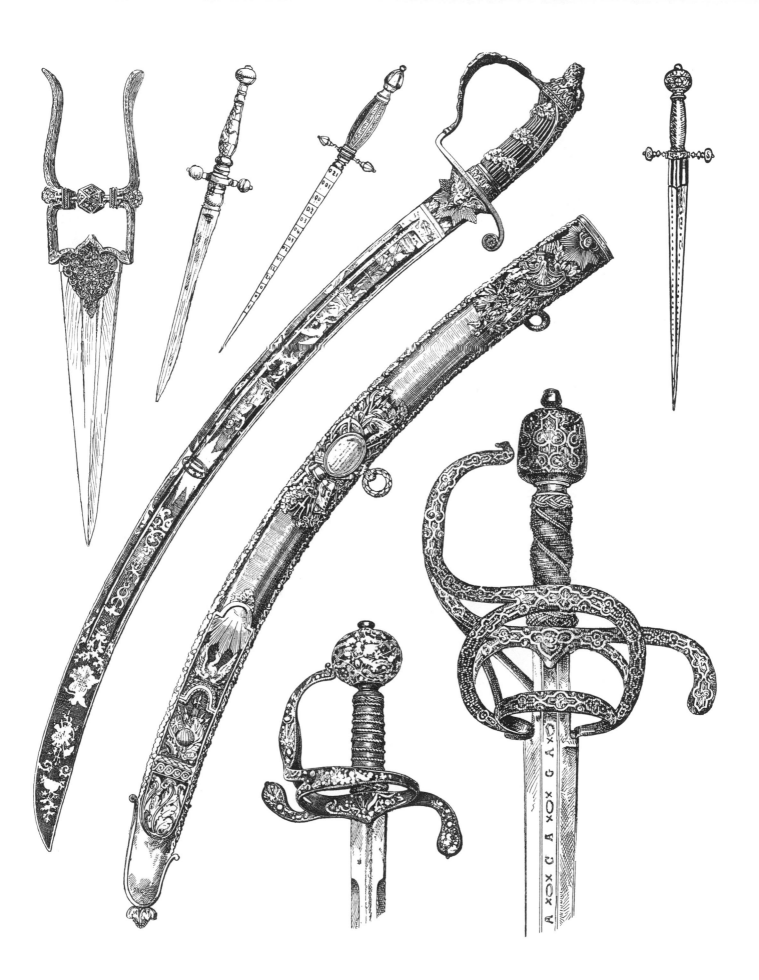

Hindu, English, Italian and unspecified *(16th- and 17th-century).*

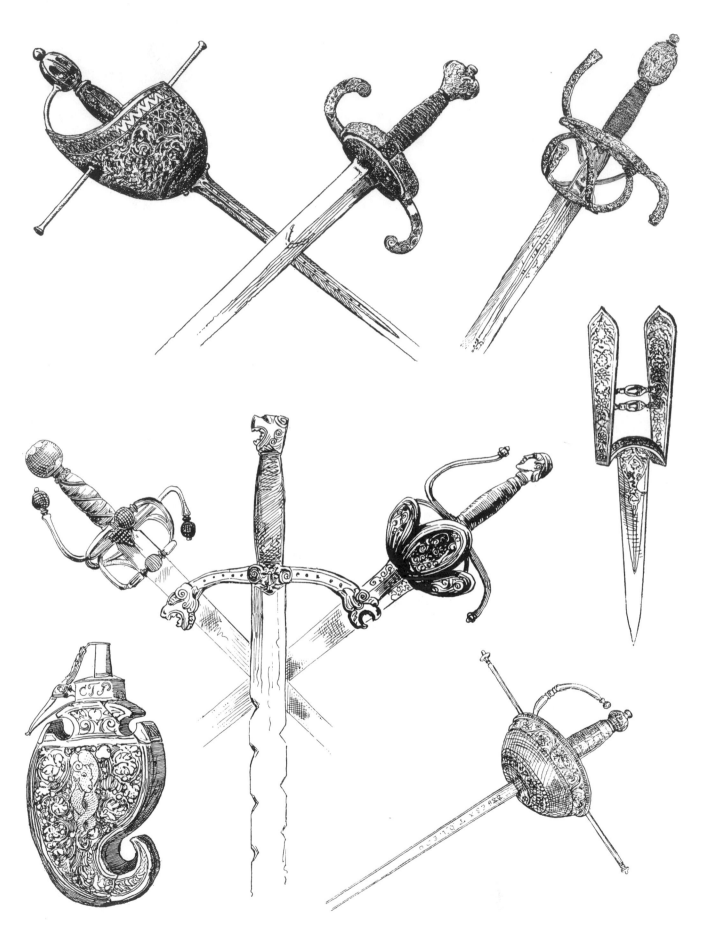

Portuguese and unspecified *(16th-century)*; English, Spanish, Hindu and
unspecified *(16th- and 17th-century)* and Italian *(17th-century)*.

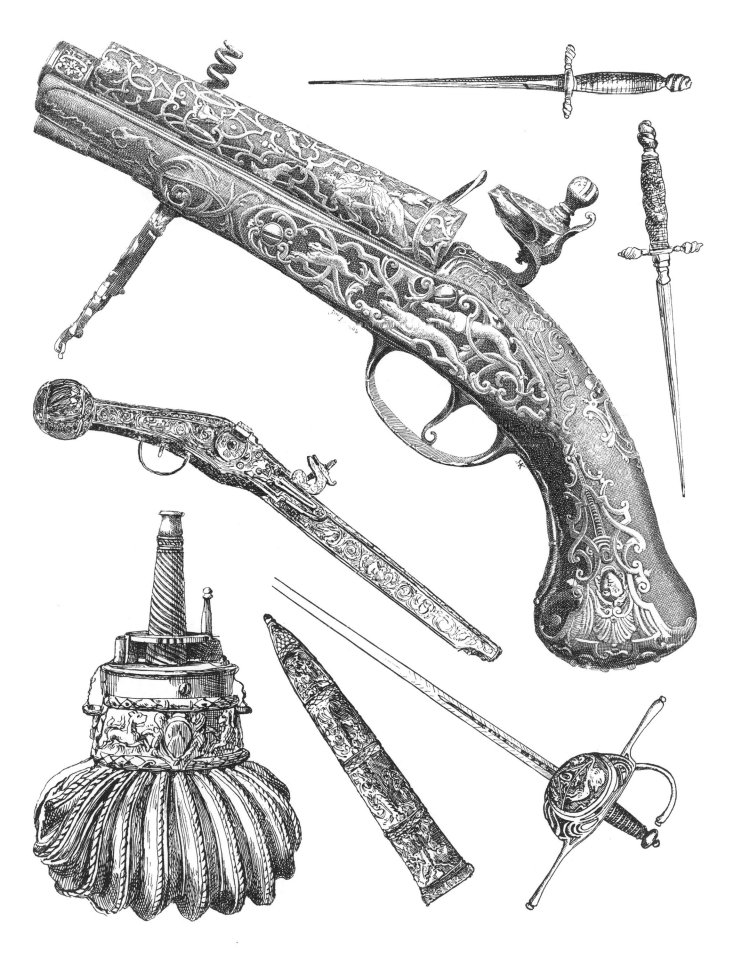

German and English *(16th- and 17th-century).*

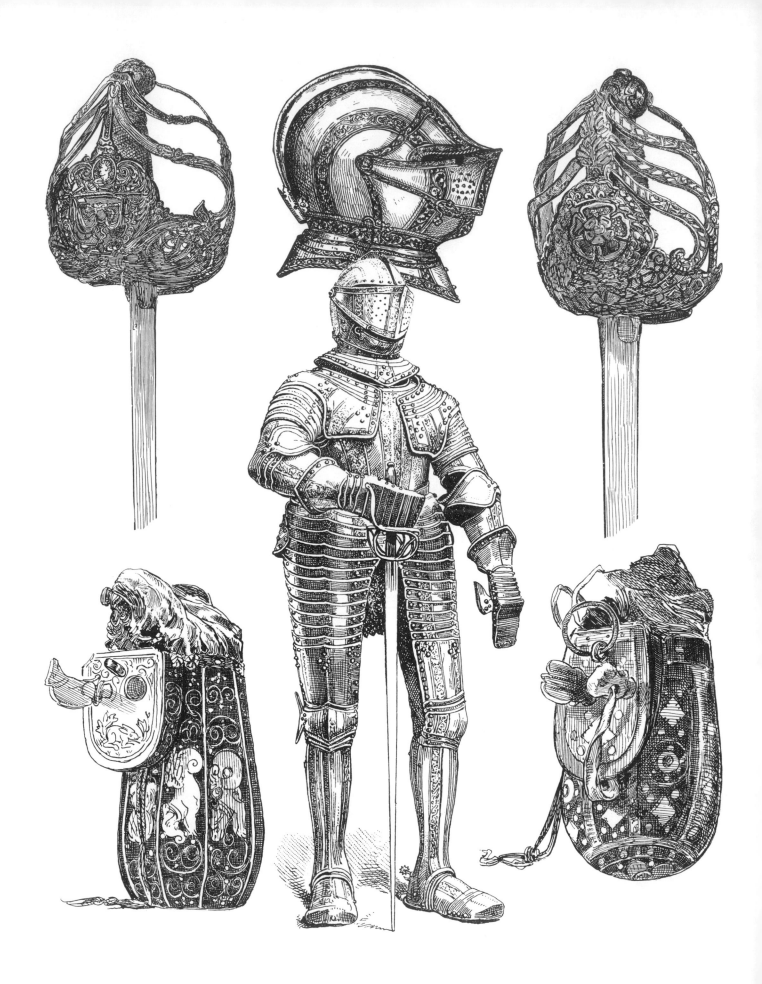

100   Italian, English and unspecified *(17th-century)*.

English and unspecified (17th-century).

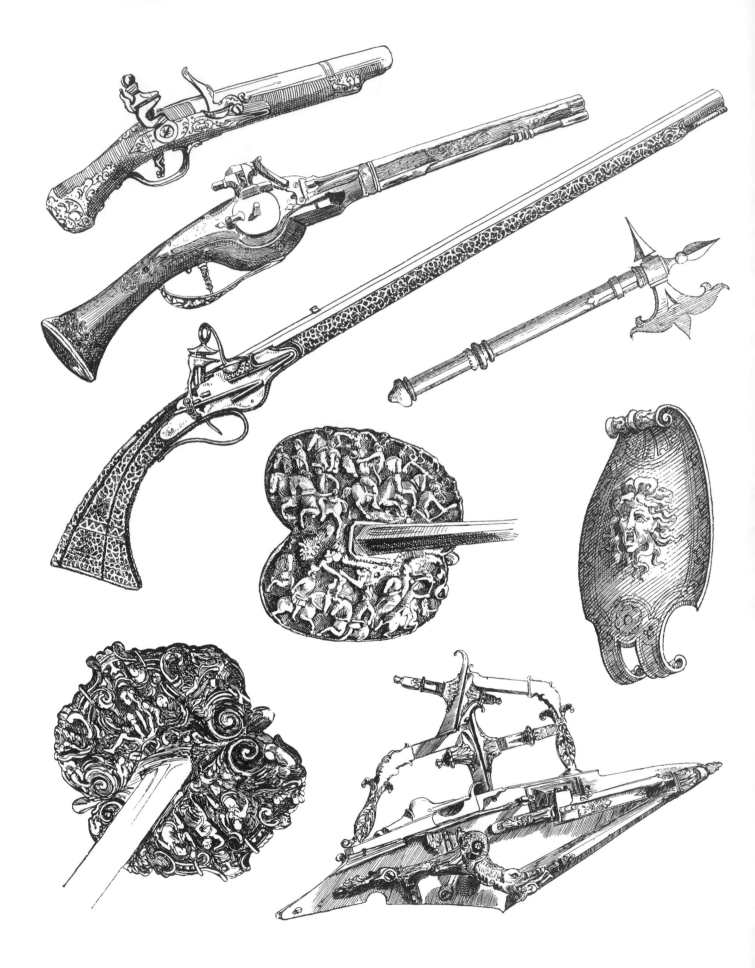

English, French, Italian and unspecified *(17th-century)*.

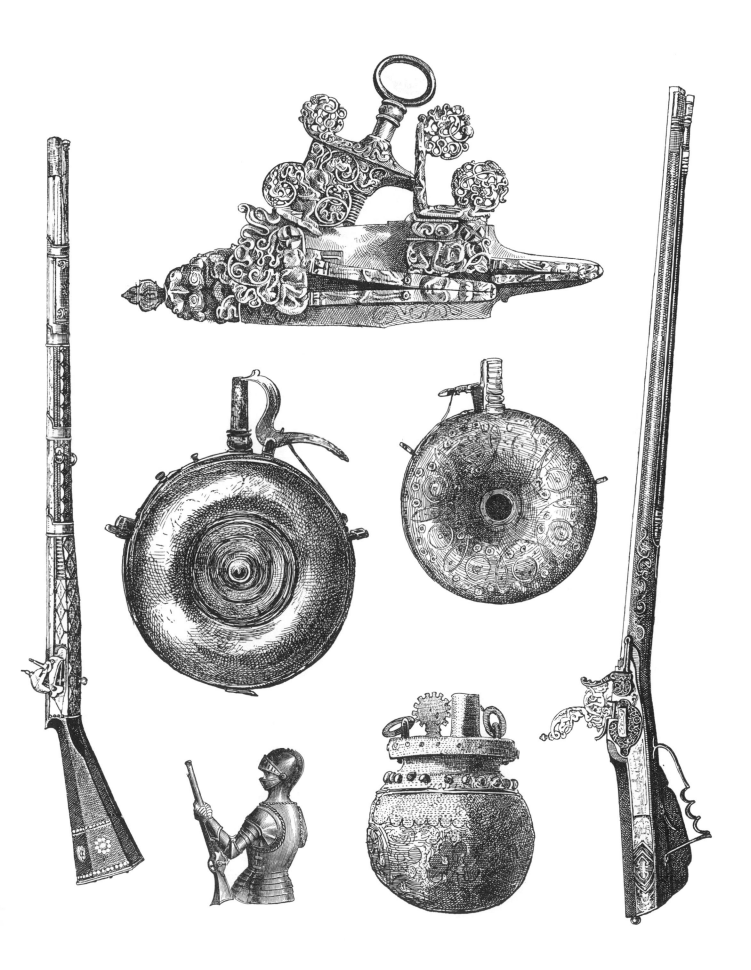

Turkish, Spanish, French and unspecified *(17th-century)*.

Italian, English, French and unspecified (*17th-century*).

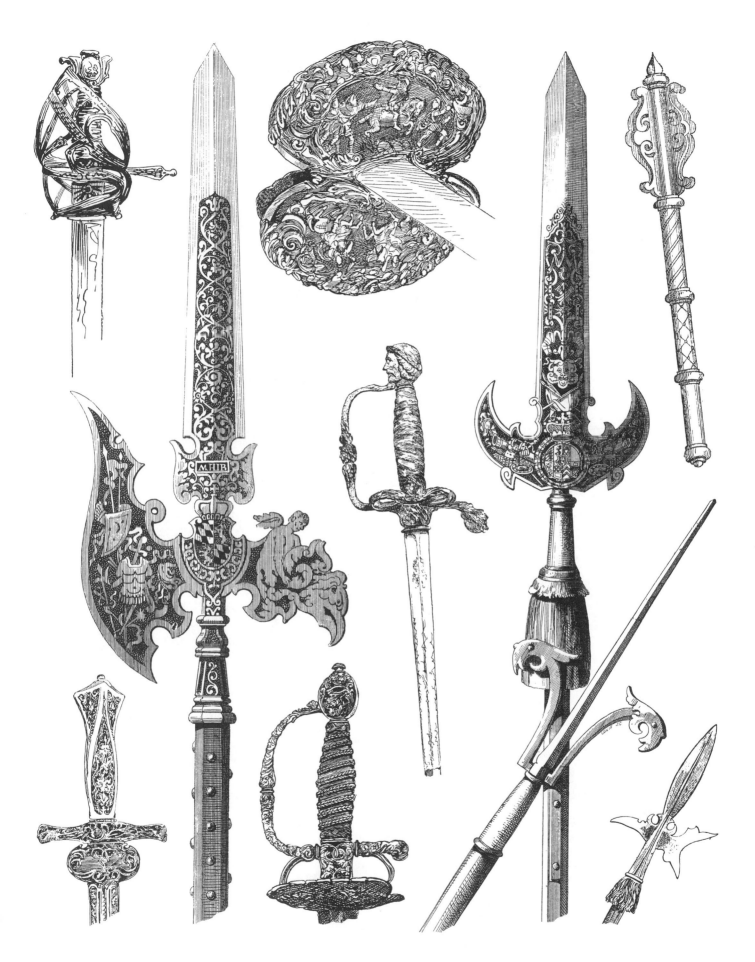

German, English, Italian, French and unspecified *(17th-century)*.

English *(16th- and 17th-century)* and Italian, Persian and unspecified *(17th-century).*

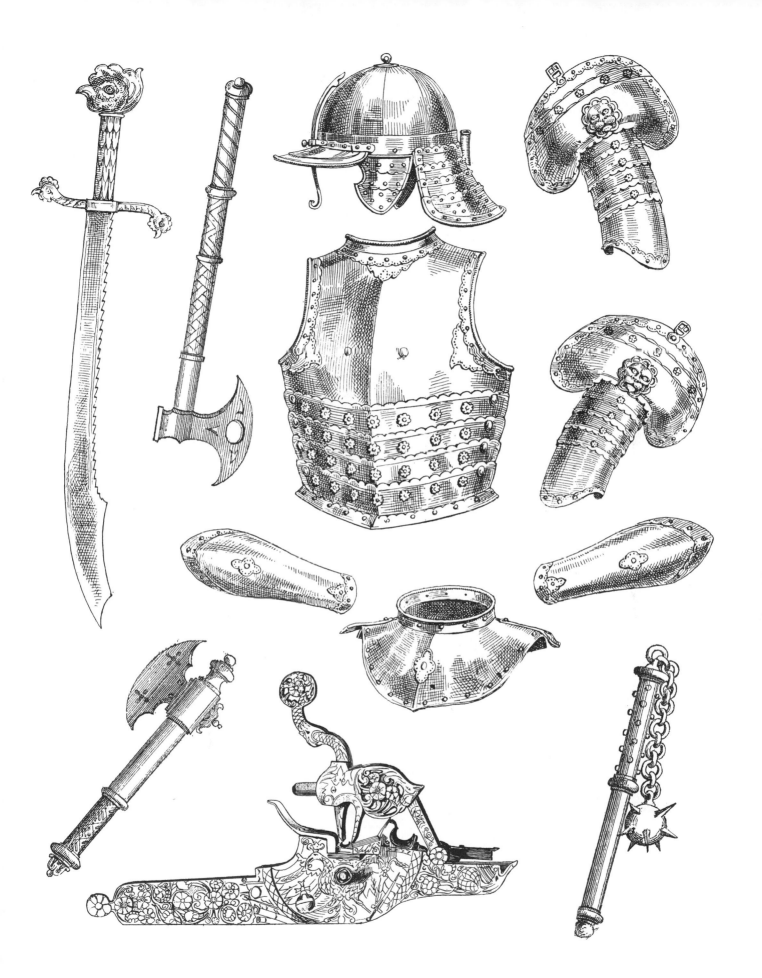

Polish, French and Austrian *(17th-century)*.

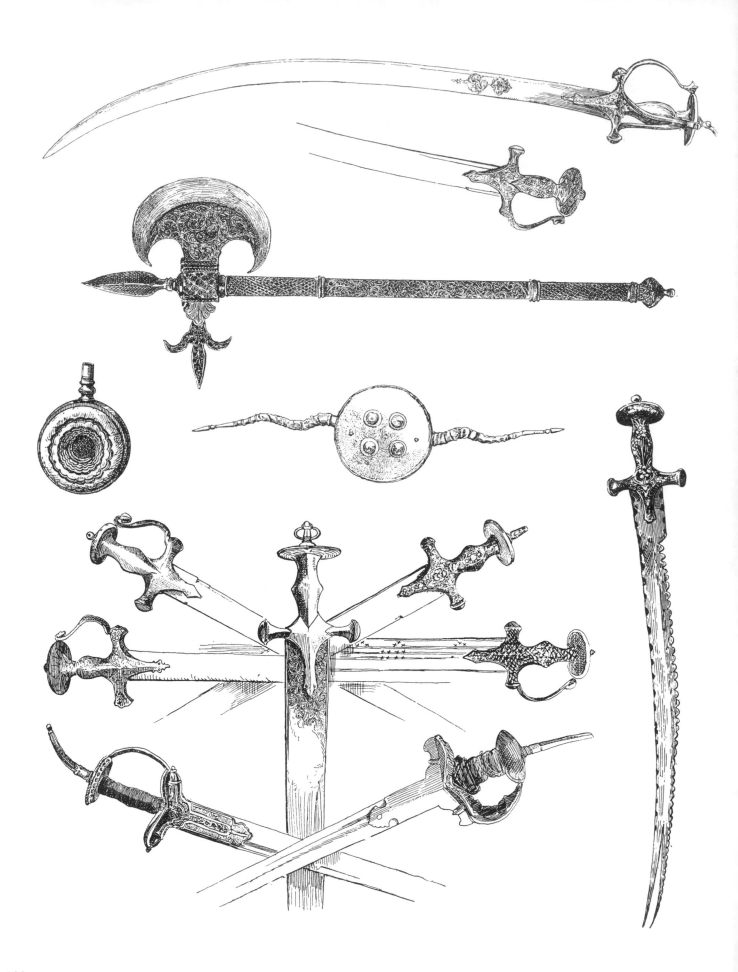

Indian and unspecified (*17th-century*).

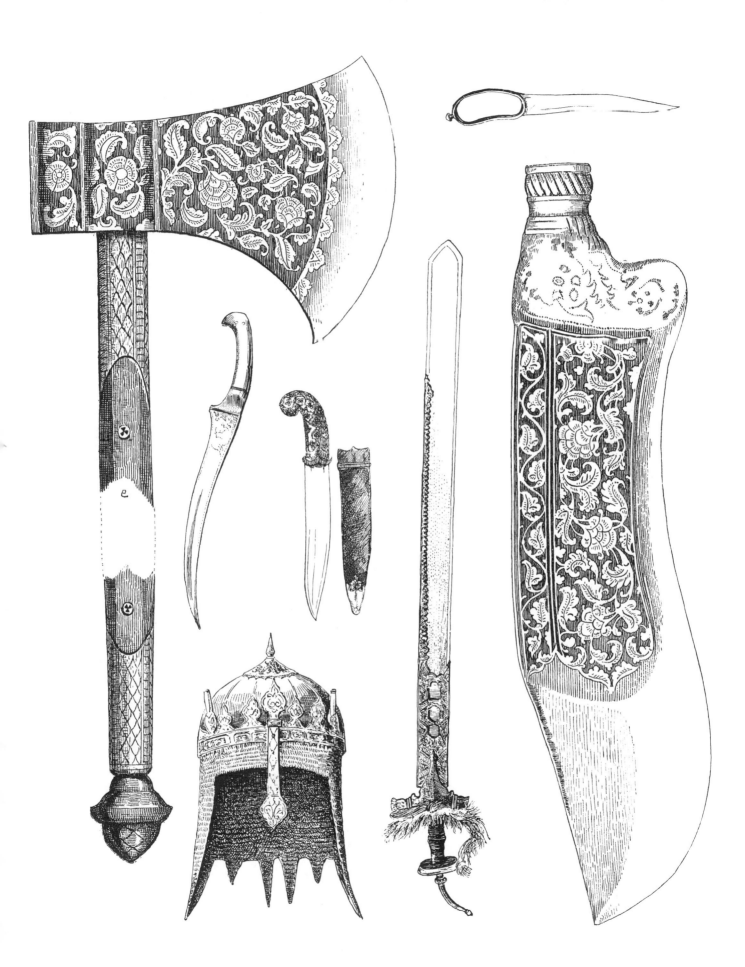

Indian *(17th-century)*.

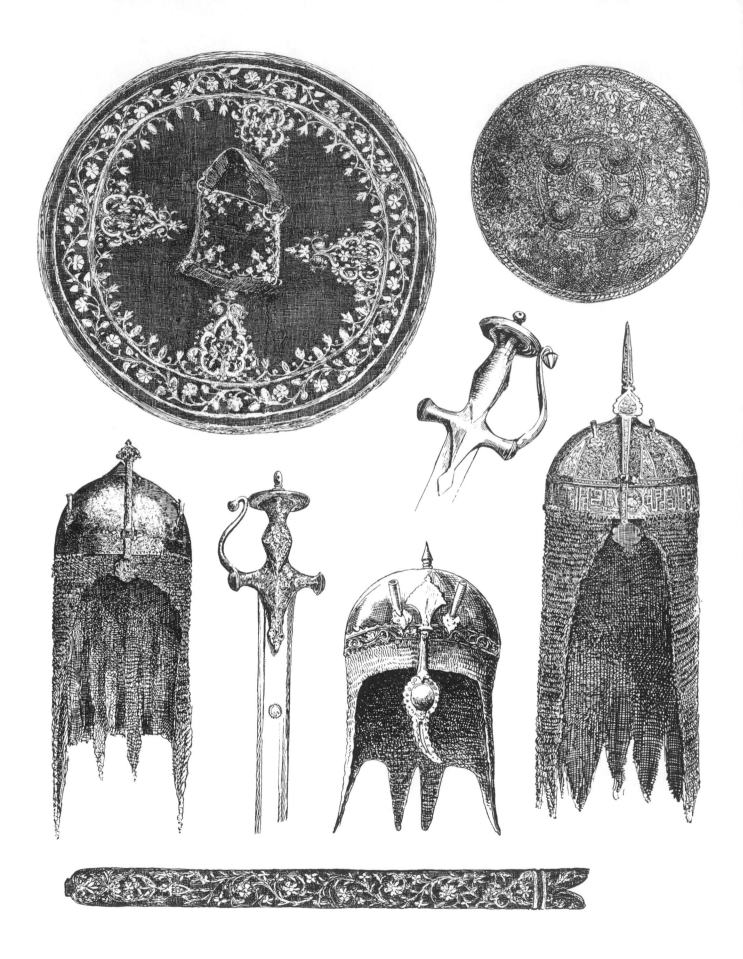

Indian and unspecified *(17th-century)*.

Indian *(17th-century)*.

Circassian, Italian, German, French and Scottish *(18th-century)*.

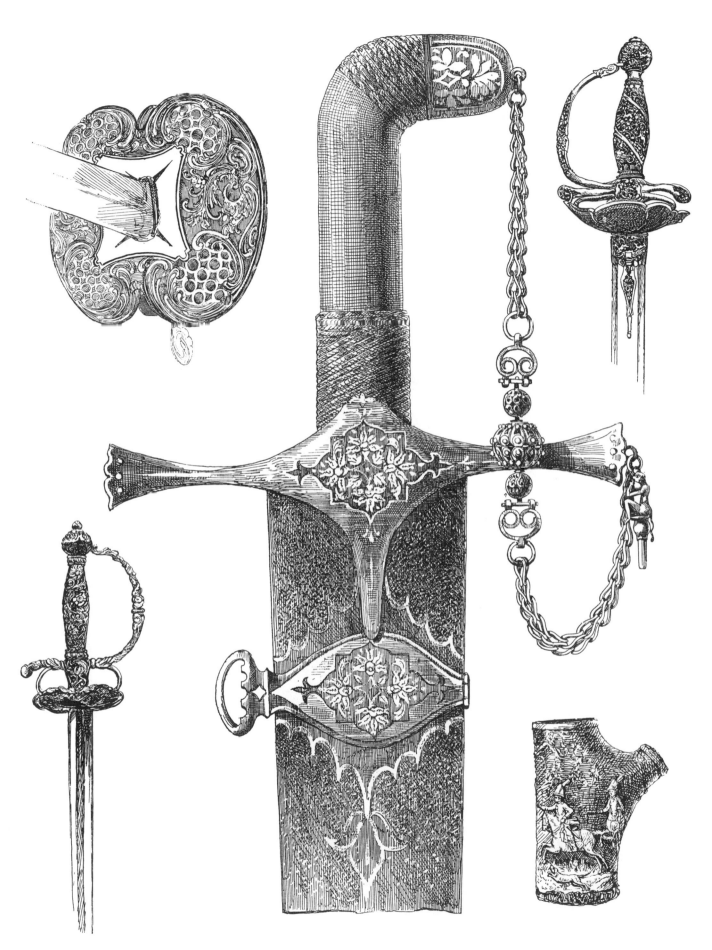

French and Persian *(18th-century).*

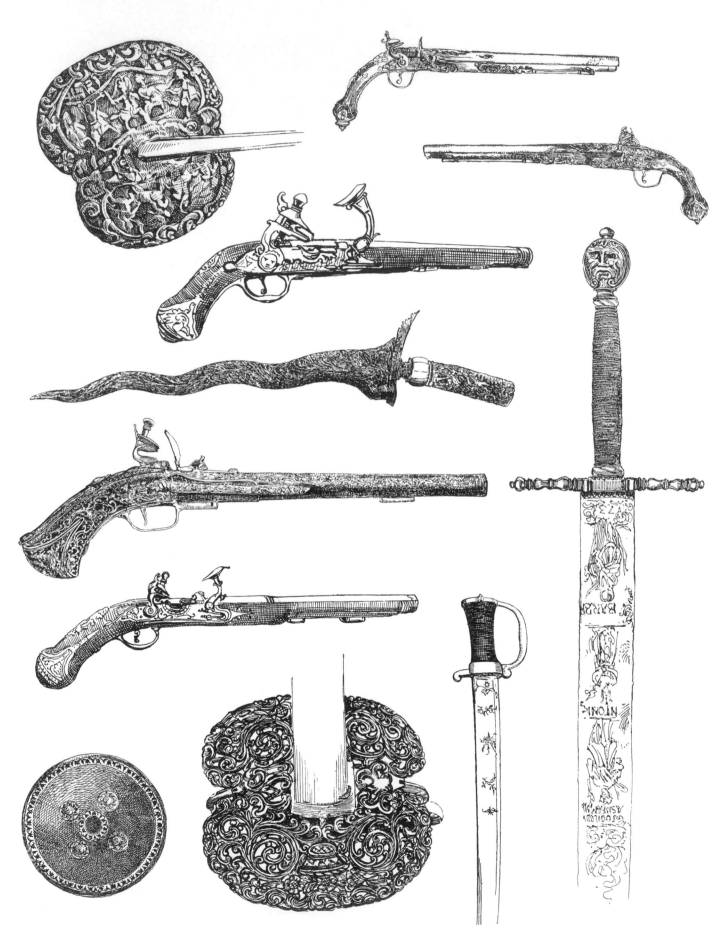

English and Turkish *(17th-century)* and Malaysian, French, Indian, Persian, German
and unspecified *(18th-century)*.

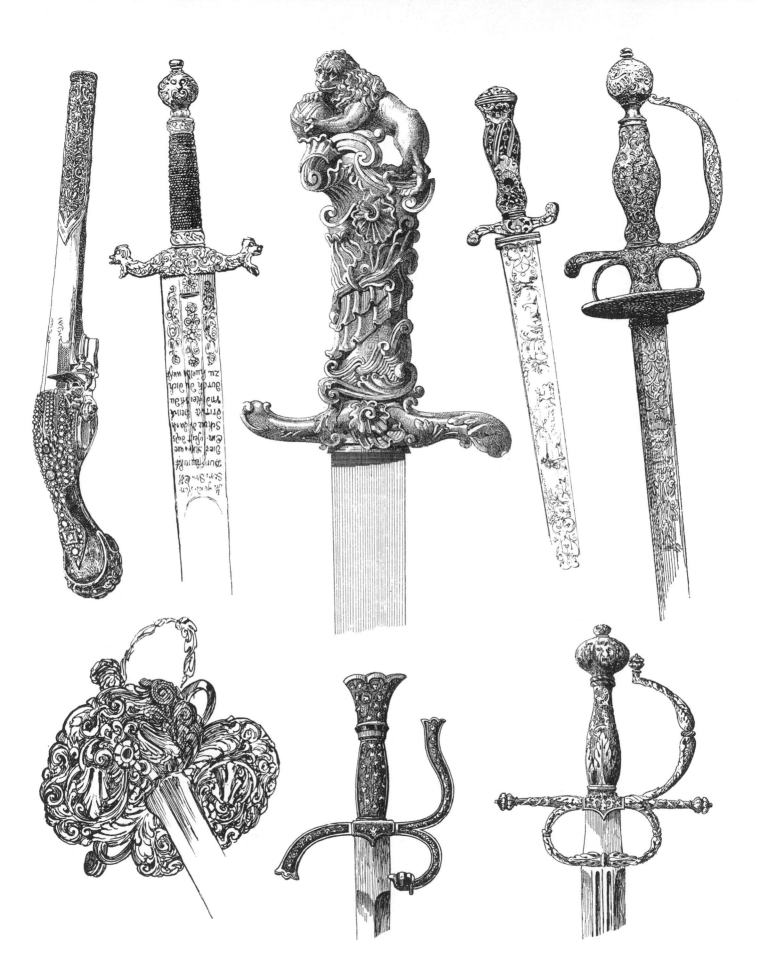

Circassian, German, French, Italian, Spanish and unspecified *(18th-century)*.

115

Unspecified decorative illustrations.

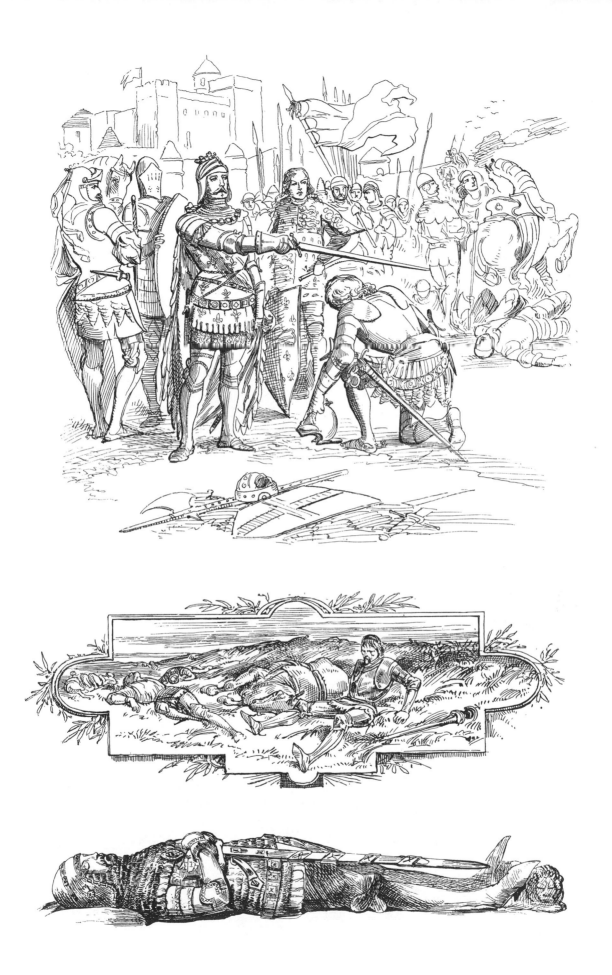

Unspecified decorative illustrations.

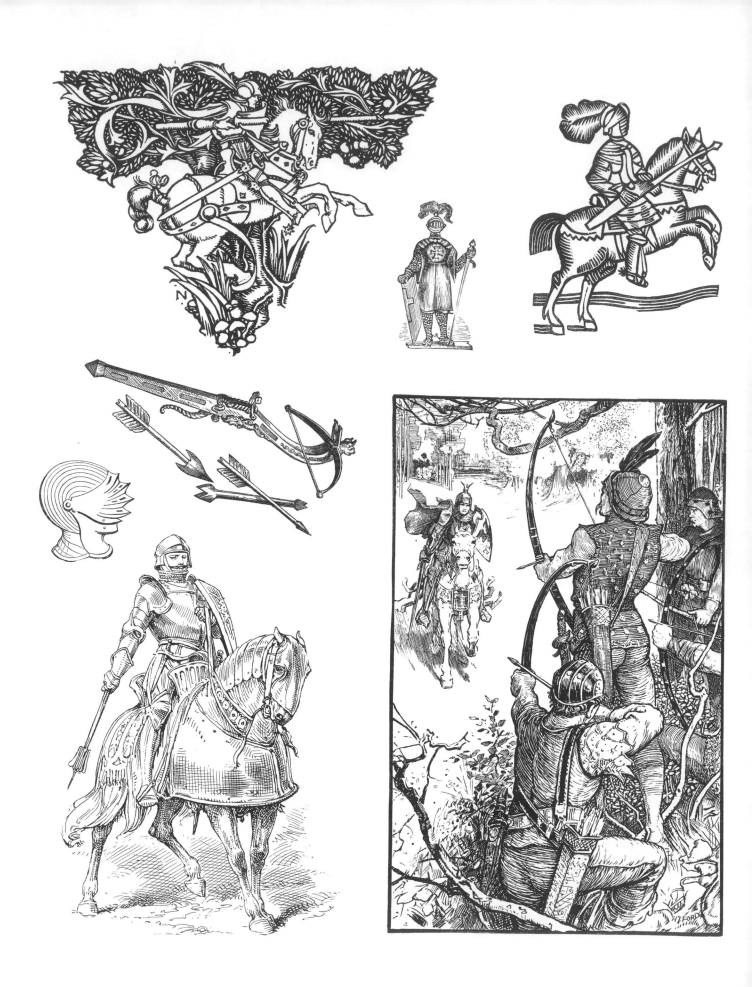

Unspecified decorative illustrations.

Unspecified decorative illustrations.